China-EU Law Series

Volume 5

More information about this series at http://www.springer.com/series/11933

Nicolas Nord • Gustavo Cerqueira
Editors

International Sale of Goods

A Private International Law Comparative and Prospective Analysis of Sino-European Relations

Springer

Editors
Nicolas Nord
Faculty of Law
University of Strasbourg
Strasbourg, France

Gustavo Cerqueira
Faculty of Law
University of Reims Champagne-Ardenne
Reims, France

ISSN 2198-2708 ISSN 2198-2716 (electronic)
China-EU Law Series
ISBN 978-3-319-54035-1 ISBN 978-3-319-54036-8 (eBook)
DOI 10.1007/978-3-319-54036-8

Library of Congress Control Number: 2017938022

Printed on acid-free paper

This Springer imprint is published by Springer Nature
The registered company is Springer International Publishing AG
The registered company address is: Gewerbestrasse 11, 6330 Cham, Switzerland

Foreword: The Chinese Law on Conflict of Laws and Its Interpretation by the Supreme Court

On 1 April 2011, the Chinese law on the laws applicable to foreign-related civil relations came into force. It is the milestone of the Chinese legislation of conflict of laws. After 2 years, the Supreme People's Court has published 'Interpretation I of several questions about application of the Law on the Laws Applicable to Foreign-Related Civil Relations' (hereinafter 'Interpretation I') on 7 January 2013. As a judge of the Supreme People's Court, today I would like to talk about the Law on the Laws Applicable to Foreign-Related Civil Relations (section "The Law on the Laws Applicable to Foreign-Related Civil Relations") and its judicial interpretation by the Supreme People's Court (section "Interpretation I by the Supreme People's Court"). But firstly, we should have knowledge of the evolution of Chinese legislation of conflict of laws (section "Evolution of Chinese Legislation of Conflict of Laws").

Evolution of Chinese Legislation of Conflict of Laws

In the first 30 years after the establishment of the People's Republic of China, the legislation of conflict of laws was a complete blank because of the lack of diplomatic activities and the echoes of nihilism. With the reform and opening up policy, international activities have been more and more, and Chinese legislators began to pay attention to conflict of laws.

In 1985, article 36 of Succession Law (published on 10 April 1985 and entered into force on 1 October 1985) and article 63 of its judicial interpretation by the Supreme People's Court (published on 11 September 1985) have provided some special rules for inheritance by a Chinese citizen of an estate outside China and the contrary situation.

In 1987, the General Principles of Civil Law (entered into force on 1 January 1987), which has always played the role of Civil Code in China, has made specially a Chapter 8 for the rules applicable to foreign-related civil relations. There are only nine articles in this chapter. Although the rules are quite few and they concern only the principles, their existence shows that the legislators began to pay more attention to conflict of laws. Then in 1988, the Supreme People's Court published 'Opinions on several questions about the application of General Principles of Civil Law (test)', in which there are 17 articles interpreting the rules of Chapter 8 of General Principles of Civil Law in relation to the law applicable to foreign-related civil relation.

Then in the following years, the Adoption Law (entered into force on 1 April 1992), the Maritime Code (entered into force on 1 July 1993), the Negotiable Instruments Law (entered into force on 1 January 1996), the Civil Aviation Law (entered into force on 1 March 1996) and the Contract Law (entered into force on 1 October 1999) have successively provided special rules on foreign-related civil and commercial relations in their respective fields. Foreign-related legislation of civil and commercial laws has entered a prosperous period.

We should notice that there are several structural parts of Chinese Private International Law: based on the relative rules of the Constitution (articles 18 and 32), the laws adopted by the Standing Committee of the National People's Congress are the main part (the General Principles of Civil Law and others) and the documents of the State Council (for example, the 'Opinions on management of foreigners' permanent residence service' of 18 February 2016 and the 'Rules on management of the permanent representative office of foreign enterprises' of 30 October 1980), each ministry and commission (for example, the 'Rules on merge and acquisition of domestic enterprises by the foreign investigators of the Ministry of Commerce of PRC' of 22 June 2009) and the local legislative documents of the provinces, cities and autonomous regions (for example, the 'Rules of Guang Dong Province on management of the contract constructions by foreign enterprises' of 14 April 1997) are subsidiary parts. According to Prof. Huang Jin, President of the Chinese Society of Private International Law, this decentralisation and diversity of Chinese legislation of Private International Law is a reflection of the progressive development of the reform and opening up policy. The Chinese legislators cannot promptly enact a Code of Private International Law in the beginning due to lack of experience, while the opening up policy imperatively needed change. At the time, the legislators had to be pragmatic by making rules in each field while dealing with relative problems in practice.[1]

[1]Jin (2011), p. 6.

The Law on the Laws Applicable to Foreign-Related Civil Relations

Firstly, I would like to talk about the legislation's background (section "Legislation Background") and then its characteristics and some regrets for the law (section "Characteristics of the Law and Regrets for the Law").

Legislation Background

We should notice that before the publication of the Law on the Laws Applicable to Foreign-Related Civil Relations, the Supreme People's Court has played a critical role in motivating the legislation of conflict of laws.

During the 30 years between 1980 and 2010, the Supreme People's Court has made lots of rules of conflict of laws by judicial interpretations and responses. The most important ones are the 'Opinions on several questions about the execution of Succession Law' of 11 September 1985, the 'Explaining of several questions about the application of Foreign-Related Economic Contract Law' of 19 October 1987 (ceased to be effective on 13 July 2000), the 'Several opinions on the questions about the application of General Principles of Civil Law (test)' of 2 April 1988, the 'Opinions on several questions about the application of General Principles of Civil Law (test)' and the 'Rules on several questions about the applicable laws in trials of foreign-related civil or commercial contract disputes' of 11 June 2007 (ceased to be effective on 8 April 2013). In fact, the last two interpretations have played a crucial role in the trials of foreign-related civil and commercial matters.

These judicial interpretations by the Supreme People's Court are very practical, applicable and manoeuvrable because they are based on situations and problems that happened in practice. In the context of unperfected legislation of conflict of laws, they have not only offered a guide to Chinese judges in dealing with foreign-related civil and commercial cases but also provided the practical knowledge for the development and improvement of the legislation.

Also, the academia has promoted the progress of legislation of conflict of laws, especially the Chinese Society of Private International Law (CSPIL). Between 1993 and 2000, Prof. Han Depei (the first president of CSPIL) has led a team to complete the 'Model law of private international law of PRC' (hereinafter 'the Model Law'). The Model Law, which combines some rules of foreign laws and opinions of Chinese academia, is a huge success and has received a lot of attention. It has incited the legislators to complete the codification of the rules of conflict of laws. The CSPIL has then dedicated itself to the Chinese legislation of conflict of laws by offering many proposals and drafts, joining the meetings of legislation debates and communicating with the People's Courts.

We should say that the communication and cooperation between the People's Courts and the academia have facilitated the final legislation by the National People's Congress.

Characteristics of the Law and Regrets for the Law

There are three characteristics of the law. Firstly, in the matters of *lex personalis*, it is the law of the place of habitual residence that applies, not the law of nationality. Secondly, the law has expanded the scope of the application of the principle of parties' autonomy of will, including marriage and family, succession, property rights and intellectual property rights. Especially, the application of the principle of parties' autonomy of will to the matters of movable property rights is creative. Lastly, in the matters of intellectual property rights, it is the law of the country where the protection is claimed. It is in line with international practice at present.

Of course, I have also some regrets for the law.

The first one is that it concerns only foreign-related civil relations, so the rules of conflict of laws in commercial relations like the rules of Maritime Law, Negotiable Instruments Law and Civil Aviation Law are not included.

The second one is that some judicial interpretations by the Supreme People's Court have not been adopted. For example, to determine the validity of arbitration agreement, according to article 18 of the Law on Laws Applicable to Foreign-Related Civil Relations, the parties may choose the law applicable and if not, 'the law of the place where the arbitration institution locates or the law of the arbitration place shall apply'. However, article 16 of the Interpretation of Arbitration Law by the Supreme People's Court of 23 August 2006 provides that the following order should apply: the law chosen by the parties, the law of the arbitration place and, in absence of the first two, the *lex fori*. In my opinion, the solution provided by the judicial interpretation is obviously better.

The third one is the absence of the definition of 'foreign-related civil relations', which is given by the Supreme People's Court in Interpretation I.

The last one is the absence of rules relative to fraud of law, previous questions and intersectional conflict of laws.

Interpretation I by the Supreme People's Court

The Law on the Laws Applicable to Foreign-Related Civil Relations came into force on 1 April 2011. Since then, the fourth civil chamber of the Supreme People's Court has begun the research on its application all over China. By the end of 2011, the fourth civil chamber has finished the 'Report on application of Law on Laws Applicable to Foreign-Related Civil Relations'. On 7 January 2013, the Supreme People's Court has published 'Interpretation I on several questions about the application of the Law on Laws Applicable to Foreign-Related Civil Relations' to provide some necessary rules in practice. I would like to talk about some of them.

The Determination of 'Foreign-Related'

The legislators were suggested to define 'foreign-related civil relations' in the text. But they thought that, firstly, the answer could be given by a judicial interpretation and, secondly, no country has defined 'foreign-related civil relations or international civil relations' in law. Hence, there is no definition of the notion of foreign-related civil relations in the Law on the Laws Applicable to Foreign-Related Civil Relations.

In the past, we determined a foreign-related civil relation through article 178 of the 'Opinions on several questions about the application of General Principles of Civil Law (test)' of 1988. According to this, foreign-related civil relation exists 'if one or two of the parties are foreigners, stateless persons or foreign legal entities; if the object of civil relation is located in a foreign country; if the facts that create, change or terminate the civil rights and obligations happened in a foreign country'. Article 304 of the Interpretation of Civil Procedure Law of 1992 has provided a similar solution.

But article 1 of Interpretation I has 'reset' the way to determine foreign-related civil relation. Based on practical experiences, we made the following modifications:

- Firstly, in article 1 §1 clause 1, we changed 'one or two of the parties are foreigners, stateless persons or foreign legal entities' to 'one or two of the parties are foreign citizens, foreign legal entities or organizations, stateless persons'. We think that the new expression is more precise.
- Secondly, it focuses no more on nationality but adds 'habitual residence' as an essential element to determine a foreign-related civil relation. So article 1 §1 clause 2 provides the situation where 'the habitual residence of one or two of the parties locates outside the territory of PRC'.
- Thirdly, we have changed 'foreign country' to 'outside the Chinese territory' in clauses 2, 3 and 4, which is more precise.
- Finally, we have provided a miscellaneous provision in clause 5 to cover other situations that may exist in practice. In fact, considering the existence of the Free Trade Zones in China, there is a tendency to include 'FTZ-related' in clause 5.

Application in Time

Article 2 provides that for foreign-related civil relations that happened before the Law on the Laws Applicable to Foreign-Related Civil Relations has come into force, the Courts should apply the relative rules applicable at the time the foreign-related civil relations happened, and in absence of which, the rules of the Law applies. That is because the rules of conflict of laws lead to the rule of law applicable to the case, and the application of the principle of non-retroactivity should apply to guarantee the expectations of the parties.

Principle of Autonomy

Article 3 of the Law on the Laws Applicable to Foreign-Related Civil Relations only provides that the parties may explicitly choose the law applicable to a foreign-related civil relation, but it does not provide when they can make the choice. During the discussion on Interpretation I, most of my colleagues think that it is reasonable to let the parties choose until the closure of the public audition of the first trial (article 8 §1 of Interpretation I). It is also in line with article 4 §1 of the 'Rules on several questions about the applicable laws in trials of foreign-related civil or commercial contract disputes' of 11 June 2007.

Article 3 of the Law on the Laws Applicable to Foreign-Related Civil Relations provides that the choice of law should be explicit. But we should notice that in practice, there exists a situation in which the parties have not explicitly chosen the applicable law in writing or verbally but during the trial they all allege the law of the same country and none of them has contested its application. In this case, the judge considers generally that they have already agreed in common to the application of this law. Thus, in Interpretation I, we have added this situation in article 8 §2.

The parties have been given so much liberty of choice that they may even choose the law of a country that has no connection at all to the issue (article 7 of Interpretation I). However, there is a limit: the parties may choose the applicable law only for matters for which the Chinese law has explicitly allowed to choose an applicable law (article 6 of Interpretation I).

Mandatory Provisions

Article 4 of the Law on the Laws Applicable to Foreign-Related Civil Relations has for the first time provided the direct application of the mandatory provisions of Chinese laws. However, it has not explained which rules are mandatory provisions.

We think that the mandatory provisions must be in favour of public social interests, to protect the national economic order or the interests of some special fields. Hence, based on judicial practices, we have given a general description of mandatory provisions and enumerated the rules that we think should be considered as mandatory provisions in article 10 of Interpretation I. They are rules on the protection of laborers' rights and interests, food safety and protection of public health, environmental safety, financial safety and protection against anti-monopoly or anti-dumping. I must point out that in our opinion, the application of mandatory provisions must be strict and prudent; the People's Courts must avoid the abuse of mandatory provisions. Until now, the Supreme People's Court has never used this rule in practice.

Application of Foreign Laws

Article 10 of the Law on the Laws Applicable to Foreign-Related Civil Relations provides firstly the obligation of the People's Courts to ascertain a foreign law. Article 193 of 'Opinions on several questions about the application of General Principles of Civil Law (test)' provides five ways to ascertain a foreign law: that is, provided by the parties, by the central department of that country with which China has established a judicial assistant agreement, by the Chinese embassy or consulate in that country, by the embassy or consulate of that country in China or by a Chinese or foreign legal expert.

The original idea of article 193 is not that the judge must try all of the five ways before declaring the impossibility of ascertainment of a foreign law. But there are many misunderstandings in practice. So article 17 §1 of Interpretation I enumerates three ways (provided by the parties, provided by the international treaties that came into force in China or provided by legal experts) to ascertain a foreign law and provides clearly that if these ways do not work, the judge may declare that the ascertainment is impossible.

Article 10 of the Law on the Laws Applicable to Foreign-Related Civil Relations also provides the obligation of the parties to provide the foreign law if they choose to apply it to the case. In this situation, we think that the judge should give them a reasonable time limit. So we provided in article 17 §2 of Interpretation I that the Court may declare that a foreign law cannot be ascertained if the parties cannot provide it within a reasonable time limit.

Intersectional Conflict

In the end, I would like to talk about the intersectional conflict of laws involving Hong Kong, Macao and Taiwan.

There are no rules in this field in Chinese laws. During the establishment of the Law on the Laws Applicable to Foreign-Related Civil Relations, we have suggested the legislative department to add the rules in the text. Unfortunately, the suggestion had not been accepted.

In practice, the judges deal with the cases involving Hong Kong, Macao and Taiwan by referring to foreign-related ones. But we obviously need the rules to invoke in our decisions. On 27 December 2010, we have published the 'Rules on applicable law in trail of civil and commercial cases in relative to Taiwan'. And in article 19, we provide that the present rules also apply to determine the 'applicable law of civil cases in relative to Hong Kong and Macao'. We can do only so much according to Chinese law.

Supreme People's Court of PRC
Beijing, China
Cheng Minzhu

References

Chunlong C (2003) Position and function of Chinese judicial interpretations. Chinese Legal Sci (1):24–32

Jin H (2011) Establishment and consummation of Chinese law on the laws applicable to foreign-related civil relations. Tribune Polit Sci Law 29(3):3–12

Wei D (2009) Reconsideration about the codification of Chinese private international law – to commemorate 10th anniversary of the establishment of "Model law of private international law of PRC". Wuhan Univ J Philos Soc Sci 2009(6):21–23

Foreword

Undoubtedly, several factors make the proceedings of the conference held in Beijing on the 20th and 21st of June 2016 a reference work: the importance of the topic is due to the intensive exchanges between China and the countries of the European Union, the broad scope of the legal questions discussed as well as the quality of the answers given by the authors of the different reports.

A special place has, of course, been reserved for the CISG which is applicable to the majority of sales contracts between China and the Member States of the European Union. However, the book also examines in depth the conflict of laws and jurisdiction rules in China and in the European Union in order to cover all aspects of relationships between Chinese and European parties. These rules are uniform in Europe, with the exception of the conflict of laws rules on international sales contracts given the coexistence of the Rome-I Regulation and the Hague Convention of 1955 to which some European states are a party. Further parts are dedicated to arbitration, the inevitable standard method for the resolution of Sino-European disputes, as well as to the Unidroit Principles of International Commercial Contracts, which arbitral tribunals may use to supplement the CISG for matters not covered by it.

The book also deals with Sino-European B2C sales contracts and the relevant conflict of laws rules, although these contracts are by far less frequent than their B2B counterparts. The discussion is, as the organisers rightfully point out, nevertheless justified by the increase of such contracts concluded online. Additionally, while European consumers will normally hesitate to initiate litigation against Chinese exporters given the considerable practical hurdles, it might be different for potential class actions initiated in Europe.

Professors Nicolas Nord and Gustavo Cerqueira announce that the topic of international sales contracts is destined to be the subject of further profound study. The general frame being established, it seems indeed that the stage is now set for the exploration of more specific aspects of sales contracts like limitation periods, the validity of limitation and exclusion clauses, the efficacy of penalty clauses, and the applicable legal interest rate, matters which are not covered by the

CISG. These are merely some examples of the many aspects of Chinese law that merit to be made known in Europe and, particularly, to be compared with the French solutions. Moreover, the rich jurisprudence of CIETAC tribunals on the CISG merits further exploration. Thus, the programme for future joint symposiums of the University of Strasbourg and the China EU School of Law is already apparent. Long live the university cooperation between Beijing and Strasbourg!

Saarland University
Saarbrücken, Germany
Claude Witz

Preface

The commercial relationship between China and the European Union has grown strong over the years. Today, the European Union is China's largest trading partner and China is the EU's second largest trading partner after the United States of America. Accordingly, international sale of goods contracts can be considered as one of the main legal tools governing the Sino-European commercial exchanges.

The main issues relating to international sales of goods contracts are well known by practitioners even though in constant evolution as trade relations between Europe and China are relentlessly growing. Despite this evolution, practitioners are often unaware of the intricacies of each legal system involved in the deals concluded and tend to learn it during litigation.

Ratified by more than 80 states in the world—including China since 2013—the United Nations Convention on Contracts for the International Sale of Goods is intended to govern a significant part of the Sino-European trade. Yet, in practice, it is far from being the case. Indeed, other national regulations and international instruments play a rather important role on this matter. Other contracts, such as consumer contracts, are excluded from the scope of this UN Convention. Furthermore, the number of these contracts tends to increase due to the development of the contracts concluded by the Internet. A double challenge exists for Europe and China: resolving the conflict of laws and protecting the consumer.

Moreover, since China's recent modernisation of its conflict of law rules, there have been new perspectives in the field of the applicable law to a contract of sale of goods that require a careful analysis.

When it comes to litigation, practitioners should also be able to choose between all dispute settlement mechanisms available. This implies to organise and coordinate these mechanisms in order to identify a competent judge or arbitrator. If arbitration is preferred, the recognition and execution of the award in the various legal systems certainly constitutes one of the key issues.

The present study is one of the first to connect the dots between European and Chinese laws by focusing on international sale of goods contracts. This collective work of European and Chinese lawyers, academics, attorneys, magistrates and arbitrators offers an unprecedented transversal and comparative legal study on the matter. As such, its main purpose is to identify the consequences of European rules on Chinese companies and vice versa, particularly regarding the issues related to the protection of consumers.

In this perspective, the chapters of this book reproduce the lectures given during the fifth symposium of the CESL—*International Symposium Series*, held on the 20th and the 21st of June 2016 at the China University of Political Science and Law, in Beijing, and jointly organised by the University of Strasbourg and the China-EU School of Law at the China University of Political Science and Law.

Far from being an end in itself, this work intends to encourage new developments that can strengthen further the relationship between China and Europe. Additional findings in the fields of international sale of goods and private international law will certainly help, thanks to comparison, to build bridges between both legal systems and business cultures.

Strasbourg, France
Reims, France
December 2016

Nicolas Nord
Gustavo Cerqueira

Contents

Part I International Sale of Goods and Conflictual Mechanisms

Identification of the Competent Judge in Europe 3
Danièle Alexandre

Identification of the Competent Judge in China 19
Xi Zhiguo

Identification of the Applicable Law in China and in Europe 25
Nicolas Nord

Part II Arbitration, an Alternative Way

International Sale of Goods: Combination of Arbitration and Mediation in China 43
Song Lianbin

Arbitration in the Field of International Sale of Goods: A French Point of View 51
Jochen Bauerreis

Integration of the Arbitral Award in the States System: Comparative Perspectives 69
Dong Jingjing

Part III International Sale of Goods and Material Solutions

The Vienna United Nations Convention on Contracts for the International Sale of Goods: Applicability, Gaps and Implementation . . . 89
Laura García Gutiérrez

The Unidroit Principles of International Commercial Contracts in the Sino-European Sale of Goods Contracts 101
Gustavo Cerqueira

Part IV International Sale of Goods and Consumers

International Consumer Sales: International Jurisdiction and ADR in Europe and China 129
Markus Petsche

The Law Applicable to Consumer Contracts: Protection and Gaps in China and in Europe 143
Nicolas Nord

Part I
International Sale of Goods and Conflictual Mechanisms

Identification of the Competent Judge in Europe

Danièle Alexandre

Trade relations between the People's Republic of China and Europe are constantly increasing, and it is then very important that actors of both sides acquire the knowledge of the legal system applied by the partner state.

I have been asked to give a contribution on the European solutions concerning identification of the competent judge when arises a dispute with regard to an international sale of goods. It is effectively necessary, first of all, to know which court has jurisdiction for the settlement of the dispute (if parties choose the judicial way) before determining the applicable law.

In Europe, nowadays (since January 2015), we have essentially to refer for this topic to Regulation (EU) n°1215/2012 of the European Parliament and of the Council of 12 December 2012 on jurisdiction and the recognition and enforcement of judgments in civil and commercial matters (recast), very often called Brussels I bis Regulation. Formerly were successively applied the Brussels Convention of 27 September 1968, replaced by Regulation (EC) n°44/2001 of 22 December 2000.

This article will be devoted to the analysis of the different heads of jurisdiction resulting from Brussels I bis Regulation in the field of international sale of goods, with a distinction between the rules of jurisdiction in the absence of a prorogation of jurisdiction and the rules of jurisdiction when there is a prorogation of jurisdiction. But it seems to me necessary to make first some preliminary remarks to facilitate the understanding of the application method of the Regulation.

D. Alexandre (✉)
University of Strasbourg, Strasbourg, France
e-mail: d.alexandre@unistra.fr

N. Nord, G. Cerqueira (eds.), *International Sale of Goods*, China-EU Law Series 5,
DOI 10.1007/978-3-319-54036-8_1

1 Introductory Remarks

I will not give details about the scope of Brussels I bis Regulation in general and will only print out some principles which govern in this Regulation the application of the jurisdictional rules and which must be known before we can do an analysis of the different heads of jurisdiction in our concerned matter.

Determination of Jurisdiction Only for Courts of a Member State of the European Union Brussels I bis Regulation (so as former texts) determines only if a court of a Member State of the European Union has or has no jurisdiction to settle a dispute. It cannot decide upon the jurisdiction of a court of a non-Member State.

Order of Examination of the Different Kinds of Heads of Jurisdiction Brussels I bis Regulation successively mentions different heads of jurisdiction. But to know whether proceedings may be brought in a court of a Member State, another order of examination needs to be used.

The first question that must be resolved (either by the plaintiff or by the seised judge) is whether an exclusive jurisdiction provided by article 24 (Chapter II Section 6) exists or not over the concerned matter, because article 24 overrides all other rules of jurisdiction (but international sale of goods is not one of the five matters mentioned in article 24).

Second, if the matter of the litigation is not concerned by an exclusive jurisdiction, the plaintiff or the judge has first to verify whether a particular rule of jurisdiction that has the objective of protecting the weaker party in matters relating to insurance, consumer contracts or individual contracts of employment (Chapter II Sections 3, 4 and 5) has to be applied, because these specific rules constitute autonomous systems, excluding in principle the ordinary rules of jurisdiction mentioned in Sections 1 and 2 of Chapter II, so as rules concerning prorogation of jurisdiction analysed in Section 7 of Chapter II (this principle of autonomy results from articles 10, 17.1 and 20.1). We must then keep in mind that when we want to determine who is the competent judge for a litigation concerning an international sale of goods, it is necessary first to examine if one of the parties is a consumer. But I have been asked to exclude from my communication consumer contracts, and you will find the needed information in Professor Markus Petsche's one (Part IV).

Third, it is only if no one of the two former categories of jurisdiction is concerned that reference can be made to the ordinary rules of jurisdiction mentioned in Chapter II Sections 1 and 2 when there is no prorogation of jurisdiction and in Section 7 when there is a prorogation of jurisdiction.

Limited Extension of Heads of Jurisdiction to Defendants Not Domiciled in a Member State Heads of jurisdiction mentioned in Brussels I bis Regulation may only be applied if the situation is an 'international one', meaning that the situation by itself links with more than one country.[1] But difference of nationality of the parties is not sufficient to attribute an international character to the situation because the nationality is not a factor that links the proceedings to the Regulation. And internationality of the situation may not result only from the choice of a foreign court.

Rules laid down in the Brussels Convention and afterwards in Brussels I Regulation were in principle only intended to establish uniform heads of jurisdiction for proceedings instituted against defendants domiciled in a Member State, while proceedings against defendants not domiciled in a Member State were governed by the domestic provisions of the forum, with some limited exceptions. The European Commission proposed for the recast of Brussels I Regulation that the Regulation's provisions for the jurisdiction of Member States' courts apply irrespective of the existence or not of the defendant's domicile in the territory of the Member State, national rules being no longer allowed to play a role in the jurisdiction of Member States' courts. But this proposal of a general extension was approved neither by the European Parliament nor by the majority of the Member States. Then article 6.1 of Brussels I bis Regulation maintains the principle that 'if the defendant is not domiciled in a Member State, the jurisdiction of the courts of each Member State shall be determined by the law of that Member State'. Brussels I bis Regulation has nevertheless increased, with regard to the former Regulation, the number of heads of jurisdiction that can exceptionally be applied even if the defendant is not domiciled in a Member State.[2]

2 Heads of Jurisdiction in the Absence of a Prorogation of Jurisdiction

I remind you that I will only analyse proceedings concerning a contract of international sale of goods where no party is a consumer. In the absence of prorogation of jurisdiction, two kinds of jurisdictional rules of Brussels I bis Regulation may apply: either general provisions mentioned in Chapter II Section 1 or special additional rules of jurisdiction mentioned in Chapter II Section 2.

[1]See CJEC 1 March 2005, Owusu, case C-281/02, declaring that a situation is considered as international not only when there are links with two Member States, but also when there are links with a Member State and a non Member State.

[2]See list in article 6.1, but I will only develop this position further, about the case of prorogation of jurisdiction.

2.1 *General Provisions on Jurisdiction*

General provisions mentioned in Section 1 are not specific for contracts, and consequently not for contracts of international sale of goods, but as they have a general scope (if we are in the material scope of the Regulation, excluding nevertheless the cases of exclusive jurisdiction and the cases where there are particular rules protecting the weaker party, as mentioned before), they can be used for proceedings concerning our matter.

Section 1 of Chapter II makes a distinction depending on whether the defendant is domiciled in a Member State or not. It is then necessary to give some preliminary indications about the concept of domicile (Sect. 2.1.1) before analysing the two cases of general provisions on jurisdiction (Sect. 2.1.2).

2.1.1 Concept of Domicile

There are two kinds of domicile that must be distinguished.

2.1.1.1 Domicile of Natural Persons

Article 62 does not give a substantive definition of this kind of domicile but mentions the law rules that have to be applied for its determination, distinguishing two different cases, either in order to determine if a party is domiciled in the Member State whose courts are seised of the matter or in order to determine if the party is domiciled in another Member State,[3] but opting in both cases for the application of an internal law.

2.1.1.2 Domicile of Companies or Other Legal Persons or Associations of Natural or Legal Persons[4]

It is said in recital 15 of the Regulation's Preamble that 'the domicile of a legal person must be defined autonomously so as to make the common rules more transparent and avoid conflicts of jurisdiction'.

Article 63.1 gives in general a substantive rule[5] offering three possibilities for the determination of the domicile of such parties; it can be the place where they have their (a) statutory seat, (b) central administration or (c) principal place of business.

---

[3]See arts. 62.1 and 62.2.

[4]Our topic is not concerned by the domicile of trusts.

[5]Another solution is adopted when the exclusive jurisdiction of art 24.2 is concerned, but it cannot happen about contracts of international sale of goods.

2.1.2 The Two Cases of General Provisions on Jurisdiction

2.1.2.1 Defendant Domiciled in a Member State (Arts. 4 and 5)

It is said in article 4.1 that 'persons domiciled in a Member State shall, whatever their nationality, be sued in the courts of that Member State'. The idea is that the domicile of the defendant is a good connecting factor to determine the competent court because it will facilitate the defence, and this rule assures a uniformity of solutions independently of the place where the defendant has his domicile if it is in a Member State.

The Court of Justice declared that this rule applies even if the plaintiff is domiciled in a non-Member State[6] and even if the dispute does not concern different Member States but only a Member State and other non-Member States.[7]

And article 5.1 adds that nevertheless those persons 'may be sued in courts of another Member State only by virtue of the rules set out in Sections 2 to 7 of this Chapter' (Chapter II).

Extra particulars are stated in articles 4.2 and 5.2 (see the articles).

2.1.2.2 Defendant Not Domiciled in a Member State (Art. 6)

Principle By virtue of article 6.1 in principle, 'the jurisdiction of the courts of each Member State shall . . . be determined by the law of that Member State'. In this case, there is no more a uniformity of solutions as in the former case, each Member State having its own solutions.

It is important to point out that article 6.2 admits that 'against such a defendant any person domiciled in a Member State may, whatever his nationality, avail himself in that Member State of the rules of jurisdiction there in force, and in particular those of which the Member States are to notify the Commission pursuant to point (a) of Article 76(1), in the same way as nationals of that Member State'. (On the opposite those specific rules may not be available when the defendant is domiciled in a Member State as it results from article 5.2).

Exceptions Article 6.1 mentions expressly four exceptions to this rule of principle, where the jurisdiction of the courts is determined regardless of the domicile of the defendant: article 18.1 concerning consumer contracts, article 21.2 concerning individual contracts of employment, article 24 concerning exclusive jurisdiction and article 25 about agreements conferring jurisdiction. But only article 25 concerns my topic and will be developed further.

We will also see later that it is generally admitted that rules concerning a defendant entering an appearance before a court of a Member State without

[6]CJEC 13 July 2000, Group Josi, case C- 412/98.

[7]CJEC 1st March 2005, Owusu, case C- 281/02.

contesting its jurisdiction mentioned in article 26 apply even if the defendant is not domiciled in a Member State.

2.2 *Special Additional Rules*

These rules are mentioned in Section 2 of Chapter II, and they are optional as the claimant has the choice between the application of these rules or the application of the general provision of article 4. They may concern either original claims (Sect. 2.2.1) or ancillary jurisdiction (Sect. 2.2.2).

2.2.1 Original Claims (Art. 7)

Article 7 enumerates seven different special additional rules, but the topic of this contribution is essentially concerned by the rules mentioned in article 7 (1) for matters relating to a contract and more particularly by article 7 (1)(b) first indent, giving full particulars about the case of sale of goods.

2.2.1.1 Scope of Article 7(1)(b) First Indent

The Court of Justice has often declared about former article 5.1 Brussels I Regulation (now article 7(1) of Brussels I bis Regulation) that the concept of 'matters relating to a contract' must be interpreted as an autonomous one (chiefly by reference to the national law of one of the Member States concerned.[8] And it is only admitted that there is a matter relating to a contract if there is an 'obligation freely assumed by one party towards another'.[9]

A question has arisen about the possibility to apply article 7(1) when the existence or the validity of the contract on which the claim is based is in dispute between the parties. The Court of Justice has admitted such a possibility when the defendant contests the existence of the contract as an incidental plea.[10] Till very recently, there was no answer from the Court of Justice for an action seeking the annulment of a contract. But a judgment of 20 April 2016[11] has decided that actions

---

[8]ex. CJEU 13 March 2014, Marc Brogsitter, case C-548/12; CJEU 20 April 2016, Profit Investment Sim SpA, case C-.366/13, §53.

[9]CJEC 17 June 1992, Handte, case C-26/91. See also the opinion of Advocate General Juliane Kokott of 2nd June 2016 in case C-185/15 §58, Marjan Kostanjevec.

[10]CJEC 4 March 1982, Effer, case 38/81 about application of the former article 5-1 of the Brussels Convention.

[11]CJEU 20 April 2016, Profit Investment Sim SpA, case C-366/13; see §58 for the decision, and §52 to § 57, but was concerned a financial contract about sale of bonds and not an international sale of goods.

seeking the annulment of a contract and the restitution of sums paid but not due on the basis of that contract constitute matters relating to a contract within the meaning of article 5(1)(a) of Brussels I Regulation.

It is important to determine exactly when the dispute concerns an international sale of goods because rules of jurisdiction are then the rules mentioned in article 7 (1)(b) first indent of Brussels I bis Regulation, which are not totally similar to the rules mentioned in article 7(1)(b) second indent for contracts of provision of services. Moreover, if the contract can be considered neither as a sale of goods nor as a provision of services, then the rules of article 7(1)(a) apply instead of the particular rules of article 7(1)(b).

Regrettably, the concept of sale of goods has not been defined in any European text. Then solutions can only be found in judicial interpretations and in comments of doctrine. It seems that to decide if the dispute concerns a contract of sale of goods, there is no difficulty when the contract only obliges a seller to deliver goods and a purchaser to pay them, but difficulties appear when the contract includes jointly supplementary obligations.

There are recent judgments of the Court of Justice about particular cases:

- CJEU 25 February 2010, Car Trim, case C-381/08, about contracts for the supply of goods to be produced or manufactured where the customer has specified certain requirements with regard to the provision, fabrication and delivery of the components to be produced. The answer to the question on the qualification of such a contract as a 'sale of goods' is as follows: 'where the purpose of contracts is the supply of goods to be manufactured or produced and even though the purchaser has specified certain requirements with regard to the provision, fabrication and delivery of the components to be produced, the purchaser has not supplied the materials and the supplier is responsible for the quality of the goods and their compliance with the contract, those contracts must be classified as a "sale of goods" within the meaning of the first indent of Article 5(1)(b) of Regulation N°44/2001' (nowadays article 7(1)(b) first indent of Brussels I bis Regulation).
- CJEU 19 December 2013, Corman-Collins, case C-9/12, about a distribution of goods agreement. The Court decides that can be considered as a 'sale of goods'... 'a long term commercial relationship between two economic operators, where that relationship is limited to successive agreements, each having the object of the delivery and collection of goods'. But the Court adds that this classification cannot be applied to 'the general scheme of a typical distribution agreement, characterized by a framework agreement, the aim of which is an undertaking for supply and provision concluded for the future by two economic operators, including specific contractual provisions regarding the distribution by the distributor of goods sold by the grantor'.

Those two decisions do not clearly define the concept of 'sale of goods', but both declare that to classify a contract in the light of article 5(1)(b) of Brussels I Regulation (nowadays article 7(1)(b) of Brussels I bis Regulation), 'the classification must be based on the obligations which characterize the contract at issue', and the second judgment adds that it is for the national court to ascertain the exact content of the contract.

2.2.1.2 Rule of Jurisdiction Resulting from Article 7(1)(b) First Indent

After mentioning in article 7(1)(a), as a rule of jurisdiction additional to the general provision of article 4, that a person domiciled in a Member State may be sued in another Member State ... ‘in matters relating to a contract, in the courts for the place of performance of the obligation in question’, it is said in article 7(1)(b) that ‘for the purpose of this provision, and unless otherwise agreed, the place of performance of the obligation shall be: in the case of the sale of goods, the place in a Member State where, under the contract the goods were delivered or should have been delivered’ (first indent; a second indent concerns the case of provision of services).

To have a more precise understanding of this particular and additional rule of jurisdiction, it is necessary to insist on two points: firstly, what contractual obligation must be considered as ‘obligation in question’ for this kind of contracts and, secondly, how will be determined the ‘place of performance’ of this obligation.

Concept of ‘Obligation in Question’ Whereas for contracts other than sale of goods or provision of services the ‘obligation in question’ is the obligation on which the claim is based, in the case of a sale of goods the ‘obligation in question’ is the obligation for the seller to deliver the goods. We can say that for this kind of contract, the ‘obligation in question’ is the characteristic one and not necessarily the real obligation concerned by the dispute: it is the obligation of delivering the goods that has always to be considered even if, for example, the dispute concerns the non-payment of the price of the goods.

But in saying ‘unless otherwise agreed’, article 7(1)(b) admits that parties shall agree to refer to the real obligation concerned by the dispute instead of the characteristic one, which may change the solution about the competent judge.

Concept of ‘Place of Performance of the Obligation in Question’ Article 7 (1) (b) gives an autonomous interpretation of the concept of ‘place of performance of the obligation in question’ and decides that ‘unless otherwise agreed’ (it means that parties shall agree to choose another place), the place of performance of the obligation in question is, for sale of goods, ‘the place in a Member State where, under the contract, the goods were delivered or should have been delivered’. The determination of the place of delivery of the goods is purely factual and does not need to refer to the law applicable to the contract.[12] Authors conclude that the United Nations Convention of 11 April 1980 on contracts for the international sale

[12]See CJCE 3 May 2007, Color -Drack, case C-386/05; CJEU 25 February 2010, Car Trim, case C-381/08; CJEU 9 June 2011, Electrosteel, case C.87/10.

of goods and particularly articles 31 and 57, which determine the place of delivery and the place of payment, has not to interfere here.

The Court of Justice has resolved some specific difficulties:

- First difficulty: if there are several places of delivery of the goods – if they are all within a single Member State, the judgment *Color Drack* opts for the principal place of delivery, which must be determined on the basis of economic criteria, and decides that 'in the absence of determining factors for establishing the principal place of delivery, the plaintiff may sue the defendant in the court for the place of delivery of its choice'.

  Remark: there is no judgment concerning a case where the several places of delivery are located in different Member States. Generally, authors are in favour of the adoption of the same solution. But some authors approve this solution only when it is possible to establish the principal place of delivery and consider, when it is not possible, that article 7(1)(b) first indent cannot be applied, reference needing then to be done to article 7(1)(a).
- Second difficulty: when the contract of sale of goods involves carriage of goods – the Court of Justice has decided in the case *Car Trim* that 'in the case of sale involving a carriage of goods, the place where under the contract the goods sold were delivered or should have been delivered must be determined on the basis of provisions of that contract. Where it is impossible to determine the place of delivery on that basis without reference to the substantive law applicable to the contract, that place is the place where the physical transfer of the goods took place, as a result of which the purchaser obtained, or should have obtained, actual power of disposal over those goods at the final destination of the sales transaction.'[13]
- Third difficulty: in case of total absence of delivery of goods – if a clause of the contract mentions the place where the goods must be delivered, it is that place that will be considered for determining the competent court.[14]

  But if there is not a specific clause, the judge has to examine the 'economy of the contract', which includes reference to Incoterms.[15]

Thanks to all those judgments, we have at the same time an answer to the question on the meaning of the expression 'under the contract' mentioned in article 7(1)(b) first indent: it can be a clause fixing that place of delivery of the goods, or in the absence of such a clause, the place of delivery can be determined in consideration of the economy of the contract and of the circumstances of the case (see *Electrosteel*).

[13]See also CJEU9 June 2011, Electrosteel.

[14]See CJEU, 25 February 2010, Car Trim.

[15]See Electrosteel.

2.2.2 Ancillary Jurisdiction (Art. 8)

Article 8 confers on a court that is seised of an action over which it has jurisdiction additional ancillary jurisdiction to entertain a related claim against a person domiciled in a Member State other than that of the court seised. These rules have been established in order to reduce the expense and the inconvenience of litigation and the risk of irreconcilable judgments. This article contains four rules concerning a person domiciled in a Member State, which have a general scope and no particularity for contracts of sale of goods. Then I will not develop this question but only mention the four cases: where the person is one of the number of defendants (art. 8(1)) or is a third party in an action on a warranty or guarantee or in any other third-party proceedings (art. 8(2)), if there is a counterclaim arising from the same contract or facts on which the original claim was based (art.8(3)), and in matters relating to a contract, if the action may be combined against the same defendant in matters relating to rights in rem in immovable property (art. 8(4)).[16]

3 Prorogation of Jurisdiction

There are two kinds of prorogation of jurisdiction mentioned in Section 7 of Brussels I bis Regulation: in case of agreements conferring jurisdiction and in case of a defendant entering an appearance before a court of a Member State.

3.1 Agreements Conferring Jurisdiction (Art. 25)

We will analyse successively the scope of article 24, the validity of the agreement and the effects of the agreement.

3.1.1 Scope of Article 25

Whereas the former Brussels I Regulation (art. 23.1) requested that at least one of the parties (even only the claimant) has his domicile in a Member State for conferring jurisdiction to the chosen court, Brussels I bis Regulation admits in article 25.1 the possibility of an agreement conferring jurisdiction regardless of the domicile of the parties. It is a very important extension of the scope of application of the Regulation (see former developments in Introductory Remarks), which demonstrates the will to increase the party autonomy admitted in a uniform way

[16]See art. 8 (1), (2), (3) and (4) for the determination of the court which has jurisdiction in each case.

by this European Regulation. But may arise a problem of interaction between Brussels I bis Regulation and the Hague Convention of 30 June 2005 on Choice of Court Agreements, which declares in its article 26(6) that 'This Convention shall not affect the application of the rule of a Regional Economic Integration Organisation that is a Party to this Convention, whether adopted before or after this Convention ... a) where none of the parties is resident in a Contracting State that is not a Member State of the Regional Economic Integration Organisation ...' (whereas, as we have mentioned, article 25.1 of Brussels I bis Regulation applies to agreements conferring jurisdiction to a court of a Member State independently of the domicile of the parties). Authors discuss about the interaction between those two texts.[17] But for the moment, the Hague Convention has a limited geographical scope,[18] and China is not yet concerned.

Article 25 of Brussels I bis Regulation only applies if the agreement confers jurisdiction to a court or the courts of a Member State (art. 25.1). If a court of a non-Member State has been chosen, then such an agreement is outside the application of the Regulation and is ruled by the private international law of this Member State or eventually by the Hague Convention on Choice of Court Agreements of 30 June 2005.

Although it is not mentioned in the Regulation, agreements conferring jurisdiction can only be submitted to article 25 if the situation for which the agreement has been concluded is an international one.[19] The French Cour de Cassation[20] mentions indirectly this necessity.

3.1.2 Validity of the Agreement

3.1.2.1 Formal Validity

The formal validity of an agreement conferring jurisdiction is admitted in three cases, mentioned in article 25.1 (a), (b) and (c).[21]

As it is said in article 25.1 of Brussels I bis Regulation that the agreement conferring jurisdiction shall be ... (a) in writing or evidenced in writing (first form possible), article 25.2 has found it necessary to specify that 'any communication by electronic means which provides a durable record of the agreement shall be

---

[17]See Gaudemet-Tallon (2015), n°129-1, pp. 143–144 and her references; Cerqueira (2016), pp. 293–295, n°15 and his references; Alexandre and Huet (2015), n°233.

[18]There are 27 and not 28 European Union States (because Denmark is excluded), plus Mexico and Singapore; United States of America and Ukraine have signed the Convention but not yet ratified it.

[19]See former developments in Introductory remarks.

[20]Cass. com. 23 Sept. 2014, Sté Compass Group Holdings, n°12-26585.

[21]There are the same as in article 23.1 of Brussels I Regulation.

equivalent to writing'. The Court of Justice has given an interpretation of former article 23.2 of Brussels I Regulation, which is equivalent to the new text.[22]

And the opinion of Advocate General Maciej Szpunar of 7 April 2016, in case C-222/15, Höszig Kft, reminds in paragraph 34 that 'the Court (of Justice) considers that the existence of an agreement (meaning a consensus between the parties) can be inferred from the fact that the formal requirements laid down in article 23.1 of Regulation N°44/2001 (nowadays article 25.1 of Brussels I bis Regulation) have been complied with'.[23]

A recent judgment of the Court of Justice[24] gives very interesting indications about how must be applied article 23.1(c) of Brussels I Regulation (nowadays article 25.1(c) of Brussels I bis Regulation) concerning the third form admitted for the validity of the agreements, but in a case were was concerned a financial contract for the sale of bonds and not a sale of goods.

3.1.2.2 Substantive Validity

To avoid parties concluding a general agreement conferring jurisdiction in any case, article 25.1 only admits agreements aiming for the settlement of 'disputes which have arisen or which may arise in connection with a particular legal relationship' between the parties. Article 25.4 mentions two categories of subject matters for which substantive validity of the agreement is restricted or prohibited, but they do not concern the topic of this contribution.

Whereas nothing was said in the former Brussels I Regulation about other conditions of validity, giving rise to many questions, article 25 of Brussels I bis Regulation has expressly given an answer to two questions formerly discussed:

- It results from article 25.1 that, to know if the agreement is null and void as to its substantive validity, it must be referred to the law of the Member State where the chosen court is located. And according to recital 20 of the Preamble, the term 'law' includes the conflict-of-law rules of that Member State (it is an alignment to the text of article 5 of the Hague Convention on Choice of Court Agreements).
- And article 25.5 mentions that 'an agreement which forms part of a contract shall be treated as an agreement independent of the other terms of the contract', adding in a second paragraph that its validity 'cannot be contested solely on the ground that the contract is not valid'.

It is generally admitted that an agreement conferring jurisdiction that fulfils all other conditions of validity cannot be considered as null only because the chosen court will not apply a policy law that would be applied by the court normally

[22]CJEU, 21 May 2015, El Majdoub, case C-322/14.

[23]This solution has been adopted by the Court of Justice for this case on 7 July 2016.

[24]CJEU, 30 April 2016, Profit Investment Sim. S.A, case C-366/13.

competent. Effectively, the law applicable and jurisdiction of courts are two questions that are separate.[25]

3.1.3 Effects of the Agreement

3.1.3.1 Nature of Effects

A valid agreement confers exclusive jurisdiction on a court or the courts of a Member State 'unless the parties have agreed otherwise' (art.25.1 of Brussels I bis Regulation). This reservation was not mentioned in the Brussels Convention but has been introduced in article 23.1 of Brussels I Regulation and maintained in Brussels I bis Regulation, showing the importance given in the Regulations to the respect of the autonomy of the common will of the parties of the contract.

When the agreement conferring jurisdiction has been concluded for the benefit of only one of the parties, the former Brussels Convention mentioned in its article 17 paragraph 5 that this party shall keep the right to bring proceedings in any other court that has jurisdiction by virtue of the Convention. That is no more indicated in the successive Regulations, but it can be admitted that this solution may be maintained as a result of the new reservation expressly mentioned in both Regulations ('unless the parties have agreed otherwise').

But there is also the more general problem of the efficiency of asymmetrical agreements conferring jurisdiction. An asymmetrical agreement conferring jurisdiction is an agreement only compulsory for one of the parties, the other one having the choice between suing the defendant in the court mentioned in the agreement or in another one competent by application of the normal rules of jurisdiction. It is also called 'imbalanced agreement'. The French courts have often been asked to resolve this question in particular cases. Two judgments of the Cour de Cassation[26] opted for the inefficiency of such agreements because they were contrary to the object and the finality of the text concerning prorogation of jurisdiction; the first one pointed out that the agreement was purely depending on the will of one of the parties, and the second insisted on the fact that the determination of the competent court was unforeseeable. A new judgment[27] has approved the court of appeal, which decided that the concerned asymmetrical agreement was efficient because it permitted sufficiently the identification of the different courts qualified to have jurisdiction, and was then in conformity with the objectives that an agreement conferring jurisdiction must satisfy. Presently, there is no judgment of the Court of Justice making decision about the efficiency of asymmetrical agreements, but it would be very useful to have one if we want a uniform solution in all Member States of the European Union, because article 25.1 of Brussels I bis Regulation submits the

[25]See Cass. com, 24 nov. 2015, n°14-14924.

[26]Cass. 1ère civ. 26 sept. 2012, n°11-26022; Cass. 1ère civ. 25 mars 2015, n°13-27264.

[27]Cass. 1ère civ. 7 oct. 2015, n°14-16898.

substantive validity of the agreement conferring jurisdiction to the law of the Member State whose court(s) has (have) been chosen, and laws may differ from a State to another.

3.1.3.2 Effects Between Parties

Parties are bound by the agreement conferring jurisdiction only for disputes that arise in matters involved in the scope of the agreement (and not, for example, for a different contract even between the same parties).

And there are new rules in Brussels I bis Regulation about lis pendens (rules concerning jurisdiction where proceedings involving the same cause of action and between the same parties are brought in the courts of different Member States) when one court is the one chosen in an agreement conferring jurisdiction.[28]

3.1.3.3 Effects Towards Third Persons

The question is if a person who did not conclude the agreement conferring jurisdiction but has links with the parties can invoke this agreement against one of the original parties or, on the contrary, if one of the original parties can use the agreement against such a person if the dispute concerns the material scope of the agreement.

A judgment of the Court of Justice[29] has declared that as one of the aims of article 23.1 of Brussels I Regulation (nowadays article 25.1 of Brussels I bis Regulation) is to ensure the real consent of the parties, 'it follows that the jurisdiction clause incorporated in a contract may, in principle, produce effects only in the relations between the parties who have given their agreement to the conclusion of that contract. In order for a third party to rely on the clause it is, in principle, necessary that the third party has given his consent to that effect.' But the Court of Justice adds that 'it is true that the conditions and the forms under which a third party to the contract may be regarded as having given his consent to a jurisdiction clause may vary in accordance with the nature of the initial contract'. And after having mentioned two kinds of contracts where a third party is deemed to have given his consent to a jurisdiction clause (but in cases not related to our topic), the Court of Justice decides that 'a jurisdiction clause agreed in the contract between the manufacturer of goods and the buyer cannot be relied on against a sub-buyer . . .

[28] See art. 31.2, 31.3 and 31.4 that I will not develop here. The rule of priority applied in general for lis pendens in favour of the court first seised (art. 29 and 30) is replaced in principle in case of an agreement conferring jurisdiction by the preference for the court chosen in the agreement if this court has already been seised.

[29] CJEU, 7 February 2013, Refcomp SpA, case C-543/10.

unless it is established that that third party has actually consented to that clause under the conditions laid down in this article' (art. 23 Brussels I Regulation).[30]

3.2 *Defendant Entering an Appearance Before a Court of a Member State (Art. 26)*

3.2.1 The Principle

Article 26.1 provides that, apart from jurisdiction derived from other provisions of the Regulation, a court of a Member State before which a defendant enters an appearance shall have jurisdiction. This article applies even if no one of the parties is domiciled in a Member State.[31]

3.2.2 Exceptions and Limitation

There are two exceptions mentioned in article 26.1: the principle shall not apply either where appearance was entered to contest the jurisdiction or where another court has exclusive jurisdiction by virtue of article 24. The Court of Justice[32] has declared that these are the only two exceptions mentioned in article 24 of Brussels I Regulation (nowadays article 26.1 of Brussels I bis Regulation), and then a tacit prorogation of jurisdiction of the court of a Member State where the defendant enters an appearance may be admitted even though the contract between the two parties contains a clause conferring jurisdiction on the court of a third country (see paragraphs 23 to 25).

A new limitation has been introduced by Brussels I bis Regulation in its article 26.2: when the defendant is the weaker party in a matter referred to in Sections 3, 4 or 5. But this question is out of my contribution and will be analysed in Part IV, which is devoted to consumer contracts.

4 Conclusion

It is undeniable that jurisdictional rules of Brussels I bis Regulation are not always very easy to be interpreted and applied. But I hope to have been nevertheless able to give you some useful indications.

[30]See, for an application by the Cour de Cassation: Cass. 1ère civ. 25 mars 2015, n°13-2476.

[31]See CJEC, 13 July 2010, Group Josi, case C-412/98.

[32]CJEC, 17 March 2016, Taser International, case C-175/15.

References

Alexandre D, Huet A (2015), Compétence, reconnaissance et exécution (Matières civile et commerciale), Rép. internat. Dalloz, Paris

Gaudemet-Tallon H (2015) Compétence et exécution des jugements en Europe. LGDJ, Paris

Cerqueira G (2016) La réduction progressive du domaine matériel du règlement Bruxelles I refondu : l'environnement normatif du nouveau règlement. Revue critique de droit international privé 2:285–307

Identification of the Competent Judge in China

Xi Zhiguo

For the solution of disputes arising out of the contracts of international sale of goods, in my point of view, to determine the competent court or courts is the first and probably the most important question to solve. The reasons are obvious. First of all, the choice of the competent court has great influence on the distribution of the litigation costs borne by the parties. In addition, to a great extent, it decides which country's procedural law, even material law, will be applied hereto and therefore determines the outcome of the actions, even the recognition and enforcement of the judgment. Fist of all, the civil procedural rules that dominate the actions are up to the competent court. Second, the court will use its own nation's laws of conflicts to decide the applicable material laws concerning the disputed contracts.

It can be also safely said to be one of the most complicated questions in the field of law of conflicts. However, just as the Hague Convention on choice of court agreements (30 June 2005) has pointed out that it is only through enhanced judicial co-operation that international trade and investment can be promoted, it is only through uniform rules on jurisdiction and on recognition and enforcement of foreign judgments in civil or commercial matters that the judicial co-operation can be enhanced. Therefore, all states and nations are making great effort to coordinate the rules of jurisdiction; the PRC is now on her way too.

Up to present, there are no specific code or rules for the proceedings to resolve international sales of goods disputes, not to mention to designate the competent courts in the system of law of the People's Republic of China. Therefore, the general rules for the civil and commercial actions involving foreign elements, which are only a part of the Civil Procedural Law of China, can be applied to this kind of disputes.

X. Zhiguo (✉)
China University of Politics and Law, Civil and Commercial Law Institute, Beijing, China
e-mail: xizhiguolaw@126.com

N. Nord, G. Cerqueira (eds.), *International Sale of Goods*, China-EU Law Series 5,
DOI 10.1007/978-3-319-54036-8_2

Not as the determination of applicable law, but there is no special or independent code for the jurisdiction over actions with foreign elements. The rules about the jurisdiction and other procedural problems are only part of the Civil Procedural Law (CPL, 4th part). In this code, only two articles (Articles 265, 266) are about the jurisdiction of civil actions with foreign elements. Just as for many of the internal civil proceedings, these two framework rules are obviously not detailed enough to solve such a complicated problem. Therefore, on 4 February 2015, the Supreme Court published a much more detailed interpretation of the CPL, which also includes interpretations for the jurisdiction over actions involving foreign elements.

Next, I will introduce the Chinese solutions to the determination of jurisdiction when the disputes arise out of international sale of goods.

1 The Priority of the Choice of Court Agreement

As in most of the jurisdictions in the world, the People's Republic of China's legal system allows the parties to choose the courts to resolve their disputes arising from contracts or other property disputes with foreign elements. This is the logical result of the principle of private autonomy. In another word, private autonomy also plays a decisive role in this field as in any other private law fields.

Generally speaking, for the determination of competent court, the choice of court agreement concluded by two or more parties has priority. If there is a valid choice of court agreement, then the chosen court has jurisdiction. The choice of court can both be express and implied.

1.1 Express Choice

It is very interesting that the newly revised CPL abrogated the rules that allow the parties to choose the court to decide their disputes involving foreign elements. According to most of the well-known scholars, the newly revised CPL's rules (Article 34 and Article 127) for the choice of court for internal actions can be directly applied to the civil actions involving foreign elements. Of course, many scholars strongly criticised this revision. Therefore, the Interpretations of the SPC (2015) adopted this principle just as before (Article 531 subsection 1). It is self-evident that the disputes arising from the contracts for the international sale of goods fall under the purview of contracts with foreign elements. Therefore, the parties can choose the competent court expressly as well as impliedly.

For the choice of court, all the following requirements must be satisfied at the same time.

The agreement must be in written form, according to the interpretations of the SPC. However, according to Article 11 of the Contract Law of China (1999), the following forms are all regarded as written forms: letters, telegraph, telex, text, fax, email, electric data exchange, etc., which are capable of expressing the will of the parties in a tangible form.

The chosen court must have some practical connections with the disputes to be submitted to exercise jurisdiction over them. These connections are only defined objectively. They can be any of the following: the domicile of the defendants or the plaintiffs, the place where the contract is signed or performed, the place where the subject matter is located. Nevertheless, it is a very complicated problem to deal with, whether or not the choice of an unrelated country's court is valid. Of course, China's court can refuse to exercise jurisdiction over actions submitted to it according to the agreement to choose China's court in cases that have no connection with the disputes. However, it is controversial, whether the choice agreement is valid, if the parties choose a third country's court that has not any connection with the disputes. Namely, can a Chinese court, which has jurisdiction according to Chinese law, decide the action regardless of the agreement?

Only one court shall be chosen. Although there is no definite or express regulation about this, according to many courts' decisions, including the Supreme Court's, if the parties choose both a people's court of the PRC and a foreign court as the competent court, the agreement is void.

The agreement shall not run counter to the exclusive jurisdiction stipulation of Chinese law. If according to the law of China Chinese courts have exclusive jurisdiction over the disputes, then the parties may not choose foreign courts to decide their disputes. Otherwise, the people's court will not acknowledge or enforce the judgment of the foreign courts. However, in the field of international sale of goods, it does not involve exclusive jurisdiction, according to the CPL of the PRC.

The agreement shall not run counter to China's forum level rules on jurisdiction. In other words, the parties can only choose the first instance courts; they may not choose the appellate courts. For the first instance of the actions, the parties may not choose a higher or lower court too.

Finally, the choice agreement shall be a valid one. Whether the agreement is valid or not should be judged in accordance to Chinese law. The choice of court agreement is one kind of contract; therefore, Chapter 4 of the Contract Law of China, which is named the validity of contract, will be applied to decide the validity of the agreement. For example, according to Article 54, if a party induced the other party to enter into a contract against its true intention by fraud or duress or by taking advantage of the other party's hardship, the aggrieved party is entitled to petition the People's Court or an arbitration institution for amendment or cancellation of the contract.

1.2 Implied Choice of Court

In a civil action involving foreign element, if the defendant raises no objection to the jurisdiction of a people's court and responds to the action by making his defence about the merits of the disputes, he shall be deemed to have accepted that this people's court has jurisdiction over the case and then the people's court shall have jurisdiction over the dispute.

2 The Dispositive Rules/the Rules Applicable in the Absence of Agreement

If there is no agreement to choose the court to decide their disputes related to foreign elements or the choice of court agreement is invalid, the Chinese court will directly apply the rules provided by the Civil Procedural Law of the PRC, which was recently revised on 31 August 2012. According to the CPL and the Interpretation of the SPC, the rules on jurisdiction in the absence of agreement are as follows:

- If the defendant has domicile or permanent residence within the territory of the People's Republic of China, China's court where the defendant's domicile or permanent residence is located is without doubt qualified to hear the actions.

If the defendant has no domicile or permanent residence but the contracts from which the disputes arise have material connections to the PRC, the courts of the PRC are competent to exercise jurisdiction over such disputes.

According to Article 265 of the CPL, in the case of an action concerning a contract dispute or other disputes over property right interests brought against a defendant that has no domicile or permanent residence within the territory of the People's Republic of China but the contract is signed or performed within the territory of the People's Republic of China or the subject matter of the action is located within the territory of the People's Republic of China or the defendant has its representative office within the territory of the People's Republic of China, the people's court of the place where the contract is signed or where the contract is performed or where the subject matter of the action is located or where the defendant's representative office is located shall have jurisdiction. According to Article 235 of the CPL, if the defendant has distrainable property within the territory of the People's Republic of China, the courts of the PRC may exercise jurisdiction over the actions brought against it. However, this kind of jurisdiction is highly controversial among Chinese scholars. Many famous scholars in China are totally against it. Some scholars suggest that there should be some limitation to this kind of jurisdiction. Namely, only when the distrainable property is enough to cover the damages or other obligation that may be borne by the defendant or defendants may the court where the distrainable property is located exercise jurisdiction over the disputes.

The Doctrine of Non-convenience Forum

The Supreme People's Court has expressly adopted the doctrine of non-convenience forum in its Interpretation. According to Article 532 of the Interpretation of the CPL published by the Supreme People's Court, a people's court may refuse to exercise jurisdiction over claims and notify the claimant to file actions in a more convenient court if the claims with foreign elements satisfy the following conditions at the same time:

- The defendant files an application that is more convenient for the other country's court to decide, or the defendant simply objects to the jurisdiction of the said people's court that accepted the action brought by the plaintiff.
- There is no valid agreement to choose the said people's court.
- The dispute does not belong to the exclusive jurisdiction of the PRC courts.
- The case has no influence on the PRC's interests or its citizen's, its legal person's or any other entity's.
- It is highly difficult for the people's court to determine the facts of the case and apply the law for the reason that the main facts did not happen in the territory of the PRC and that the law of the PRC is not applicable to the dispute.
- Some foreign countries'courts have jurisdiction over the dispute, and it is more convenient for them to decide the dispute.

3 The Way to Deal with Conflicts of Jurisdictions

Conflicts of jurisdiction can be divided into two categories, namely positive conflicts and negative ones. Positive conflicts mean that both a people's court and a foreign court have jurisdiction over the same disputes between or among the same parties. On the other hand, the so-called negative conflicts mean that no court is competent to decide the disputes between or among the parties.

3.1 Positive Conflicts

Now let me turn to the solution to positive conflicts. When both a people's court of the PRC and a foreign court have jurisdiction over the same dispute between the same parties, how will the people's court decide whether it accepts the claim brought by one of the parties?

If a competent foreign court has already made a valid judgment and the judgment has already been acknowledged by a people's court, then the court will refuse to accept the same claim.

If one of the parties has already filed an action in a competent foreign court and the action is pending and the other party brings an action in a competent people's court, the people's court may exercise jurisdiction over this dispute. In this case, the judgment made by the foreign court shall not be recognised and enforced by the people's court of the PRC. Many scholars criticised this rule for the reason that it runs counter to the principle of *non bis in idem*, and it also seriously interfered with other states' judicial sovereignty. Therefore, many scholars suggest that under this circumstance, China' court shall decline jurisdiction.

As for the same party that filed an action both in China's competent court and a foreign competent court, there is no express rule. However, most of the scholars suggest that in this situation, Chinese courts should decline the action in accordance with the principle of *non bis in idem*. And most of Chinese courts also so decide.

3.2 Negative Conflicts

Finally, I must point out that in theory, there are some cases over which no courts have jurisdiction,which are the so-called negative conflicts of jurisdiction. In judicial practice, however, this kind of conflict never happened as I know. Therefore, no rules have been made to resolve negative conflicts of jurisdiction. And I think there is no need to study this in detail.

4 Conclusion

It is very complicated to decide the competent court for international sale contract disputes in China just as in any other jurisdictions. This article only provides a framework on this topic. It is very useful to point out that there are two elements that play the most important roles, namely the autonomy of parties and the public interest of China.

Further Reading

1、李旺,《当事人协议管辖与境外的判决与执行法律制度的关系初探》,载于《清华法学》, Vol.7,No.3(2013)
2、甘勇,《涉外协议管辖:问题与完善》,载于《国际法研究》,Vol. 4 (2014)
3、杜焕芳,《涉外民事诉讼协议管辖条款之检视》,载于《法学论坛》,No. 4, July (2014)
4、李旺,《国际民事裁判管辖权制度析》,载于《国际法研究》, No. 1 (2014)
5、黄进主编,《国际私法》(第二版),法律出版社2005年版,北京

Identification of the Applicable Law in China and in Europe

Nicolas Nord

The comparison between the European and Chinese solutions concerning the identification of the applicable law to international sale of goods contracts is more and more easy. Both systems have now codified their rules for the determination of the law applicable to international contracts, including the sale of goods.

In China, the Law of the People's Republic of China on the Laws Applicable to Foreign Civil Relations, adopted by the Standing Committee of the National People's Congress on 28 October 2010 is concerned. It is the first time since the foundation of the People's Republic of China in 1949 that China adopts a global text in the field of Conflict of Laws. The text came into force on 1 April 2011. All the contracts concluded after this date are submitted to the new Statute.

In Europe, Regulation n°593/2008 of the European Parliament and of the Council of 17 June 2008 on the Law applicable to contractual obligations, called Rome I, must be applied to all the contracts concluded after 17 December 2009.[1] All the Member States are concerned, except Denmark. It is not the first text trying to unify the solutions between the Member States. The contracts concluded before are submitted to the Convention on the Law applicable to contractual obligations opened for signature in Rome on 19 June 1980, which is in force in all the different Member States.[2] It must also be mentioned that the Hague Convention of 15 June 1955 on the Law applicable to international sales of goods has been signed and ratified by Denmark, France, Finland, Italy and Sweden. According to article 25 §

[1]Article 28: **Application in time** "This Regulation shall apply to contracts concluded after 17 December 2009".

[2]For the contracts concluded before the entry in force of the Convention, the conflict-of-law rules of each State are applicable. The date of entry in force of the Convention is not the same for the different member States but they are all parties. For more details, see for example, Gaudemet-Tallon, Fasc. 552-11, n°16 and 35.

N. Nord (✉)
Faculty of Law, University of Strasbourg, Strasbourg, France
e-mail: nicolas.nord@unistra.fr

N. Nord, G. Cerqueira (eds.), *International Sale of Goods*, China-EU Law Series 5,
DOI 10.1007/978-3-319-54036-8_3

1 of Rome I, this Convention takes precedence over the Regulation. This is also true for the Rome Convention, according this time to its article 21. If a judge from one of these countries knows of a case, he will then apply the solutions of the Hague Convention.

A common point must be underlined: there is no definition, neither in the Chinese Statute nor in the European texts, of the notion of contract or of the sale of goods. This means that even if the codifications can be considered as a progress, they are not exhaustive and that the knowledge of the judicial solutions still remains important.

Beyond this single observation, a more global convergence phenomenon exists and will be demonstrated. The codification is, in that way, an essential element because it allows a better readability, and so a better comparison, of the rules determining the law applicable. Such a similarity is of course important and reassuring because it permits to avoid different results according to the court that knows of the case. The continuity of legal relations and international harmony are essential, especially in the field of sale of goods. In case of disharmony, the risk can be considered as too important for the potential parties. It could be an obstacle to the development of the commercial relations between Europe and China.

In both systems, the autonomy of the will is the solution of principle. The parties have the possibility to choose the law applicable to their international contract (Sect. 1). If such liberty is not used, a law objectively applicable must be identified. Despite apparent differences, the solutions are again very close (Sect. 2).

1 Possibility to Choose the Applicable Law

The general conflictual solution is the same and is easy to understand. The determination of the applicable law depends on the will of the parties (Sect. 1.1). Beyond this convergence concerning this general solution, the implementation, even if not identical, is similar in both systems (Sect. 1.2).

1.1 The Same Conflict-of-Law Rule in Europe and in China

In Europe and in China, there are no particular solutions for sale of goods contracts. The general conflict-of-law rules must be used. We will first focus on the European solution (Sect. 1.1.1) and then on the Chinese one (Sect. 1.1.2). The advantages of such a flexible rule will also be underlined (Sect. 1.1.3).

1.1.1 The Possibility of Choice in Europe

The solution can be found in Regulation Rome I. According to its article 3 § 1, entitled 'Freedom of Choice', 'A contract shall be governed by the law chosen by the parties'.

The same solution can also be found in Rome's Convention of 1980, the ancestor of the Regulation,[3] and in many private international laws of the Members States before, applicable to the contracts concluded before the entry into force of the Convention.[4] The solution is nowadays no more in question in Europe.[5]

1.1.2 The Possibility of Choice in China

The same solution is proclaimed by article 41 of Law on the laws applicable to foreign related civil relations of 28 October 2010. According to its first sentence, 'The parties may by agreement choose the law applicable to their contract'.

Just like in Europe, such a solution is not a novelty. It has been admitted, as a general solution, by the law on contracts of 1999. According to article 126, '[p] arties to a foreign related contract may select the law applicable for resolution of a contractual dispute, except as otherwise provided by law'. Even before, such a solution has been introduced in different special laws.[6]

1.1.3 The Advantages of the Solution

In Europe, legal certainty and predictability are at the forefront. The 'preamble' of the Regulation is significant. Thus, its overall objective, according to recital 16, is to ensure 'legal certainty in the European judicial area'. This is why 'the conflict-of-law rules should be highly foreseeable'. To achieve this result, '[t]he parties' freedom to choose the applicable law' is adopted and 'should be one of the cornerstones of the system of conflict-of-law rules in matters of contractual obligations'.[7]

The situation is the same in China. Of course, texts are not as explicit as in Europe. But the doctrine justifies the use of autonomy in the same manner.[8]

This means that in both systems, the parties can make a choice, and even if a problem arises many years after, they know which law must be applied to solve it or, in case of litigation, which law will be used by the judge.

---

[3]Article 3 "Freedom of choice" "1. A contract shall be governed by the law chosen by the parties".

[4]Giuliano and Lagarde (1980), p. 15.

[5]The same approach can be found in article 2 of the 1955 Hague Convention.

[6]Mellone and Nord (2013), p. 154.

[7]Recital 11.

[8]Zhang (2006), p. 315 and the references; Wang (2009), p. 3.

The convergence of the main principle is remarkable and important in practice. It means that a choice of law can be admitted before the courts of both systems. The choice of the judge is not determinant concerning the freedom of choice. Of course, the question of its implementation is then essential. For that question also, a rapprochement can be demonstrated.

1.2 *A Similar but Not Identical Implementation*

The European legislation, though not exhaustive, is detailed and provides many information on the choice of the applicable law. Article 3 of Rome I Regulation includes five paragraphs that reflect the general principle in a detailed way. In the Rome Convention, four paragraphs concern the choice, also in article 3. On the contrary, the Chinese text proclaims general principles, without going beyond. Article 41 of the new Statute of 2010 has only one sentence. This means that the analysis must be based, in China, on the Interpretations of the Supreme Court that fill the legal vacuum left by the Chinese laws.

It is of course not possible to consider that the European solutions must automatically be applied in the same way in China. The general principle is certainly the same, but it should be applied taking into account the specificities of the Chinese legal system and more generally be adapted to the Chinese reality.[9] The legal regime cannot be perfectly identical to that prevailing in other systems. Three particular aspects, the main ones, will be studied. This will permit to prove that despite some originalities, the global approach is the same.

1.2.1 Choice of Parties and Restrictions on National Laws

The leeway of the parties to an international contract should be identified and more specifically which rules can be elected.

In Europe, there is no hesitation. In the presence of a stipulation designating the *lex mercatoria*, for example, the judge must consider that there is no choice made by the parties. He should then use the conflict-of-laws rules applicable in the absence of choice.[10] Article 3 of Rome I Regulation and the Rome Convention use the word 'law'. This means, according to P. Lagarde, that the texts have not considered the possibility of choosing a non-State rule.[11]

The approach is a very narrow one. This is why some inflexions can be found in the recitals of Regulation Rome I. First of all, according to recital n°13, 'This

[9]Zhang (2006), p. 294 and more generally, Li-Kotovtchikhine (2010), p. 947.

[10]Art. 4 Rome Convention and Regulation Rome I.

[11]Lagarde (1991), p. 287, n°19. The same solution is applicable for the 1955 Hague Convention, its article 2 using also the word "Law".

Regulation does not preclude parties from incorporating by reference into their contract a non-State body of law or an international convention'. Non-national rules are not ousted, but their real signification will be determined by the *lex contractus*, identified by the conflict-of-law rule applicable in the absence of choice.

Then recital n°14 provides that 'Should the Community adopt, in an appropriate legal instrument, rules of substantive contract law, including standard terms and conditions, such instrument may provide that the parties may choose to apply those rules'. The proposal for a regulation of the European Parliament and of the Council on a Common European Sales Law is considered here.[12] Such an instrument could be identified as a 'Law' according to article 3. But the destiny of this proposal is uncertain. It will probably never be transformed into a regulation. It also means, *a contrario*, that it is the only exception. Other non-State sources cannot be chosen by the parties.

In China, the issue is more controversial. The word 'Law' was used systematically in the various texts, before the 2010 Statute. This means that, just like in Europe, an organic reference was made. The Interpretations of the Supreme People's Court may also be invoked. Thus, according to article 1 of the SPC Interpretation on related Issues concerning the Application of Law in Hearing Foreign-Related Contractual Dispute Cases Related to Civil and Commercial Matters of June 11, 2007, 'The law applicable to foreign-related contracts related to civil and commercial matters refers to the substantive law in related countries or regions, excluding the conflict of law and procedural law'.[13] The solution this time appears explicitly. There is no place left for commercial customs or codification of uses.

It seems, however, that the Law of 2010 has changed the Chinese solutions. The parties' leeway appears to be more important now. According to the most famous authors, article 3 must be interpreted as permitting the designation of international customs or international conventions.[14] The solution is reinforced by article 9 of the Court's Interpretation of 10 December 2012,[15] according to which 'Where the parties in their contract refer to an international convention which is not effective in the PRC, the People's Court may determine their rights and duties pursuant to it, unless its provisions violate the socio-public interests or the mandatory rules contained in laws and administrative regulations of the PRC'.

The parties may therefore refer, to govern their contract, to an international convention, which is not yet in force in China. This is then clearly a non-State rule because it has not or not yet been included in the Chinese system. That confirms, *a fortiori*, that the Unidroit principles or Incoterms, for example, can be chosen by the

---

[12](COM(2011) 635 final). For comments, see Schulze (2012), Deshayes (2012).

[13]See already before, article 2(2) of the responses of the People's Supreme Court to questions arising out of the application of the Foreign Economic Law of October 19, 1987.

[14]Pissler (2012), p. 10; Huang and Jiang (2011), p. 12.

[15]Interpretation on Several Issues concerning the Application of the "Law of the People's Republic of China on the Application of Laws to Foreign-Related Civil Relations". For comments, see Leibküchler (2013), p. 88, Huo (2013), p. 685.

parties. Such a solution is defended by the doctrine for several years.[16] This question will also be developed by other speakers tomorrow. This is why I will not say too much about it.

1.2.2 No Requirement of a Connection Between the Chosen Law and the Legal Relationship

The texts are silent in both systems. Despite this shortcoming, the solutions adopted appear to be quite the same. In Europe, the solution is clear and well accepted. The chosen law may be neutral and be elected specifically for that. The doctrine is unanimous on this point.[17] A contract between a Chinese and a French firm concerning goods in China to be delivered in France can be governed by the English law chosen by the parties.

In China, the issue has been discussed for a long time in the literature. According to earlier works, 'most Chinese private international law scholars are of the view that the law chosen by the parties should have some connection with the contract'.[18] According to more recent articles, the issue is still debated in the absence of a response by the legislator.[19] As for the latest articles on the subject, they indicate a general consensus in the literature regarding the admission of the designation of a neutral law by the parties to an international contract.[20]

The Statute on private international law may be invoked to strengthen the latter opinion. Indeed, the possibility to choose the law is repeatedly proclaimed by the legislator, even outside the strict area of contracts. However, in some articles, there are restrictions and only some laws, exhaustively listed, may be chosen. Article 41, general provision in the field of contracts, does not provide for such restrictions. Therefore, this means, conversely, that complete freedom is given to the parties and that any law can be designated. Article 7 of the 2012 Interpretation of the SPC confirms the solution and not only for contracts. Parties can choose a law that has no connection with their civil relationship. According to this text, '[w] here a party contends the invalidity of a choice of law by invoking the absence of any real connection to the law chosen by agreement with the legal relationship in question, that argument is not supported by the people's courts'.

---

[16] Xiao and Long (2009), p. 201.

[17] Lagarde (1991), p. 287, esp. n°20; Jacquet, n°47 et s.; Gaudemet-Tallon, Fasc. 552-15, n°7; see before Curti-Gialdino (1972), 751 s., n° 53 and the references.

[18] Xu (1989), p. 650.

[19] Zhang (2006), p. 321.

[20] Xiao and Long (2009), p. 197.

1.2.3 Concept of Choice

In Europe, the texts are intentionally written in a flexible manner. According to article 3 of Rome I Regulation, the choice shall be made 'expressly' or 'clearly demonstrated by the terms of the contract or the circumstances of the case'. Even with different words, the solution was the same in the Rome Convention.[21] This reflects the previous practice of most European States.[22] The same idea can be found in the Hague Convention.[23] If a law is systematically invoked in the correspondence between the parties and quoted in different articles of their contract, an implicit choice could be admitted. An example is even given by recital n°12 of the Regulation, according to which 'An agreement between the parties to confer on one or more courts or tribunals of a Member State exclusive jurisdiction to determine disputes under the contract should be one of the factors to be taken into account in determining whether a choice of law has been clearly demonstrated'.

In China, an explicit choice of law seems to be imposed by article 3 of the 2010 Statute. 'The parties may **explicitly** choose the law applicable to their foreign-related civil relation in accordance with the provisions of this law.'

This provision confirms a classical solution in China. The same approach has also been retained by article 3 of the Interpretation of the Supreme Court of 11 June 2007,[24] in article 2 (2) of the responses of the SPC to questions arising out of the application of the Foreign Economic Law of 19 October 1987 and by the Model Law of Private International Law of the Chinese Society of Private International Law in its article 100.[25]

It seems, however, that the Chinese system gradually goes in the same direction as Europe. Some relaxation can be demonstrated.

The first clue is that the procedural behaviour of the parties can be taken into account. Thus, according to article 8 § 2 of the 2012 Interpretation of the SPC, 'When all parties invoke the law of the same country and did not oppose the application of this law, the people's courts may consider that the parties have chosen the law applicable to their civil relationship with a foreign connection'. The same solution can be found in the 2007 Interpretation. According to Article 4, '[t]he people's court shall permit the parties concerned to choose a law or alter a choice of law applicable to contractual disputes by agreement prior to the end of court debate of the first instance.

[21]Article 3§1 second sentence: "*The choice must be expressed or demonstrated with reasonable certainty by the terms of the contract or the circumstances of the case*".

[22]Guiliano (1977), p. 215.

[23]According to article 2§2, "*Such designation must be contained in an express clause, or unambiguously result from the provisions of the contract*".

[24]"*To choose a law or alter a choice of law applicable to contractual disputes shall be done by the parties in an explicit manner*". See Li-Kotovtchikine (2002), p. 151.

[25]The text of the "Model law of private International law of the people's Republic of China" (Sixth draft, 2000) is published in the *Yearbook of Private International Law*, Vol. 3, 2001, 349.

In case the parties concerned fail to choose a law applicable to contractual disputes but both invoke the law of a same country or region and neither has raised any objection to the choice of law, the parties concerned shall be deemed as having made the choice of a law applicable to contractual disputes.'

It can be considered as a kind of procedural agreement;[26] both parties can implicitly agree by pleading on the basis of the same law.

These solutions have been admitted, even before, by the judges. In some cases, the courts have admitted implicit choices for many years, resulting mainly from the procedural behaviour of the parties.[27] They do not stick to the narrowest interpretation.

The second clue can be found in the doctrine. Some authors plead for a more general approach. According to Pr Huang and Du, it is possible to be faced in practice with situations where no doubt exists as to the desire of the parties to designate a particular law, even if there is no explicit choice. Such intent may be inferred from the particular circumstances in which the contract has been concluded, the content of it or the behaviour of the parties.[28] The authors justify this approach by a comparative law study. They especially invoked the Swiss law on private international law (1987), Rome I Regulation and the Rome Convention, the Inter-American Convention of 1994 on the law applicable to contracts and the Hague Convention of 22 December 1986 on the Law Applicable to Contracts for the International Sale of Goods.

Even with such a flexible approach, parties do not always make a choice. This lack is sometimes caused by a simple oversight or by the absence of knowledge of such a possibility. In other situations, parties do not manage to achieve an agreement on this point. This means that subsidiary solutions must be identified.

2 The Law Applicable in the Absence of Choice

We will try to prove that, despite the appearances, there is, in both systems, a special conflict-of-law rule (Sect. 2.1), which is only a presumption because it can be ousted by an exception clause, based on the principle of proximity (Sect. 2.2).

[26] In France, see Cass. Civ. 1ère 6 May 1997, n° 95-15.309, *Bull. civ.* I, n° 140; *Rev. Crit. DIP* 1997, 514, n. B. Fauvarque-Cosson.

[27] See some decisions *in* Huang and Du (2005), p. 672 and *in* Xiao and Long (2009), pp. 198–199.

[28] Huang and Du (2005), p. 672 et s.; Xiao and Long (2009), p. 198.

2.1 *The Existence of Special Conflict-of-Law Rules*

To understand the texts, we need to start with the analysis of the European solutions (Sect. 2.1.1). The Chinese approach will then be easier to study (Sect. 2.1.2).

2.1.1 Special Conflict-of-Law Rules in Europe

The Rome Convention must be considered as the point of departure. According to its article 4 § 1, 'To the extent that the law applicable to the contract has not been chosen in accordance with Article 3, the contract shall be governed by the law of the country with which it is most closely connected'. This principle cannot be used as such. It is far too general. This is why a presumption has been introduced in § 2: '[...] it shall be presumed that the contract is most closely connected with the country where the party who is to effect the performance which is characteristic of the contract has, at the time of conclusion of the contract, his habitual residence, or, in the case of a body corporate or unincorporate, its central administration. However, if the contract is entered into in the course of that party's trade or profession, that country shall be the country in which the principal place of business is situated or, where under the terms of the contract the performance is to be effected through a place of business other than the principal place of business, the country in which that other place of business is situated.'

Such a solution was problematic for some contracts, such as franchise or distribution contracts, because it is difficult to identify the 'performance which is characteristic of the contract'. To simplify the reasoning, special rules have been introduced in article 4 § 1 of the Regulation for eight contracts, the main ones. The sale of goods is concerned by two of them.

> To the extent that the law applicable to the contract has not been chosen in accordance with article 3 and without prejudice to articles 5 to 8, the law governing the contract shall be determined as follows:
>
> (a) A contract for the sale of goods shall be governed by the law of the country where the seller has his habitual residence.[29]
>
> (g) A contract for the sale of goods by auction shall be governed by the law of the country where the auction takes place, if such a place can be determined.

In the first situation, the performance that is characteristic is, this time, identified by the text itself. In the second, the mechanism by which the sale is organised seems to be predominant. The solutions seem to be easier to use now. But another question

[29]The solution is the same in article 3 of the 1955 Hague Convention according to which: "*In default of a law declared applicable by the parties under the conditions provided in the preceding article, a sale shall be governed by the domestic law of the country in which the vendor has his habitual residence at the time when he receives the order. If the order is received by an establishment of the vendor, the sale shall be governed by the domestic law of the country in which the establish ment is situated*".

appears: what can be considered as a contract of sale of goods according to this provision?

Part of the answer can be found, once again, in the recitals. According to number 17 'As far as the applicable law in the absence of choice is concerned, the concept of "provision of services" and "sale of goods" should be interpreted in the same way as when applying Article 5 of Regulation (EC) n° 44/2001 in so far as sale of goods and provision of services are covered by that Regulation'. This means that there is no direct definition either in Regulation Rome I or in Regulation Brussels I. The solutions must be found in judicial interpretations, especially the judgments of the Court of Justice of the European Union and must be coherent from an instrument to another. The explanations given by Pr Alexandre for conflict of jurisdictions can be used for conflict of laws.

2.1.2 Special Conflict-of-Law Rules in China

The Chinese system seems to be on the Rome's Convention level, a general rule including all contracts.[30] According to the second sentence of article 41 of the 2010 Statute, 'Absent any choice by the parties, the law of the habitual residence of a party whose performance of obligation is most characteristic of the contract [...] shall be applied'.

The European experience, the Convention and clarification by the Regulation could be used for the interpretation of this article concerning the sale of goods. Again, the seller could be considered as the party whose performance of obligation is most characteristic. The solution would be the same as the one given by the SPC, in article 5 of the Interpretation of 2007, even if the basis is different. According to this provision, the principle is that 'In case the parties concerned fail to choose a law applicable to contractual disputes, the law of the country or region with the closest connection thereto shall be the applicable law'. This solution comes directly from the second sentence of article 126 of the Contract Law of 1999. The most interesting point comes just after. A list of special conflict-of-law rules for 17 contracts can be found. It is a concretisation for each type of contract of the principle of proximity.

The contract of sale is the first of that impressive list:

> (1) As for contracts of sale, the applicable law shall be the law of domicile of the seller at the time of contract conclusion. In case a contract is concluded after negotiation at the domicile of the buyer, or the contract clearly prescribes that the seller shall fulfill the consignment obligation at the domicile of the buyer, the law of domicile of the buyer shall be the applicable law.

This means that, just like in Europe, in principle, the application of the law of the State in which the 'party whose performance of obligation is most characteristic' is the expression of the general principle of proximity. It should lead to the application

[30] About the question in general, Tu and Xu (2011), p. 179.

of the law of the domicile of the seller. Of course, a new interpretation could be given on this point by the SPC.

In both systems, this is only the first step of the reasoning. The second one concerns the principle of proximity, used this time as an exception.

2.2 *The Principle of Proximity as an Exception Clause*

The texts in Europe have already been interpreted by the Court of Justice, but the solutions are still obscure (Sect. 2.2.1). In China, the wording of article 41 of the 2010 Statute is ambiguous. The comparison with the European system could clarify the situation (Sect. 2.2.2).

2.2.1 The Exception Clause in Europe, an Obscure Mechanism

In Europe, the exception can be found in § 3 of article 4 of Rome I Regulation: 'Where it is clear from all the circumstances of the case that the contract is manifestly more closely connected with a country other than that indicated in paragraphs 1 or 2, the law of that other country shall apply.' The Rome Convention contains the same solution in article 4 § 5: 'Paragraph 2 shall not apply if the characteristic performance cannot be determined, and the presumptions in paragraphs 2, 3 and 4 shall be disregarded if it appears from the circumstances as a whole that the contract is more closely connected with another country.'

Such an exception is not used very frequently. Some decisions have been given by the Court of Justice, not in the field of international sale of goods but concerning international contracts of carriage[31] or individual employment contracts.[32]

According to the Court, the clause 'must be interpreted as meaning that, where it is argued that a contract has a closer connection with a country other than that the law of which is designated by the presumption laid down therein, the national court must compare the connections existing between that contract and, on the one hand, the country whose law is designated by the presumption and, on the other, the other country concerned. In so doing, the national court must take account of the circumstances as a whole, including the existence of other contracts connected with the contract in question.'[33] This means that a real comparison must be made between the law designated by paragraph 1 and the law that is alleged to have a closer connection with the contract. Systematically, the law that is considered to be

---

[31]CJEU 6 October 2009, Intercontainer Interfrigo SC (ICF) v. Balkenende Oosthuizen BV, MIC Operations BV, C-133/08.

[32]CJEU 12 September 2013, Anton Schlecker v. Melitta Josefa Boedeker, C-64/12.

[33]CJEU 23 October 2014, Haeger & Schmidt GmbH v. Mutuelles du Mans assurances IARD (MMA IARD), C-305/13.

the closest one must be applied. All the connections should be taken into account. The conclusion is that no real hierarchy appears between paragraphs 1 and 2 and paragraph 3 in the motivation of the Court. They are all at the same level. The result is a complete lack of previsibility.

The introduction of the adverb 'manifestly' in the Regulation may change the reasoning, introducing a real hierarchy between the paragraphs and the necessity to interpret the escape clause restrictively. The law designated by paragraph 1 would then be applicable, except if another is obviously the closest one. But there is no interpretation by the Court of Justive or by a national supreme court yet.

2.2.2 The Exception Clause in China, an Ambiguous Wording

In China, the text itself is difficult to interpret. The wording is ambiguous because the conjunction 'or' is used.[34] Two alternative solutions seem to exist in that article and are at the same level. It seems to be impossible to argue that there is a principle and an exception: 'Absent any choice by the parties, the law of the habitual residence of a party whose performance of obligation is most characteristic of the contract or the law that most closely connected with the contract shall be applied.'

In opportunity, the alternativity would, of course, be a very bad solution as we have seen it in Europe. Many questions appear immediately and cause different problems of interpretation. It would then be much more convincing to consider that 'the law of the habitual residence of a party whose performance of obligation is most characteristic of the contract' is an expression of the principle of proximity, which must be considered as the principle.

But opportunity is not law. This is why another argument must be found. Article 5 of the SPC Interpretation of 2007 may again be used. The construction of this article is interesting and significant.

Proximity is the principle, in the absence of choice: 'In case the parties concerned fail to choose a law applicable to contractual disputes, the law of the country or region with the closest connection thereto shall be the applicable law.' The method to be used is then mentioned: 'When determining the law applicable to contractual disputes in accordance with the principle of using that with the closest connection, the people's court shall determine the law of the country or region having the closest connection with the contract as the applicable law of a contract in light of the particularities of the contract and that the performance of contractual obligations by one party concerned can best embody the essential characteristic of the contract, etc.'

The list of 17 contracts can then be found. And finally, according to the last sentence, 'In case any contract above is of obvious and closest connection to another country or region, the law of the country or region shall prevail'.

---

[34] Cerqueira and Nord (2011), p. 88.

This means that proximity is the main principle. The different special conflict-of-laws rules can be considered as presumptions. If the principle of proximity is not satisfied by these presumptions, they must be ousted.[35] But the closer connection must be 'obvious'. Even if the wording is not the same, it reminds the adverb 'manifestly' introduced in Rome I Regulation. The escape clause is then an exception and must be interpreted restrictively.

Of course, it is difficult to consider that the 2010 law can be explained by a former interpretation. But a kind of continuity could then be demonstrated, which is essential in that particular field. We are still waiting for the interpretation of the SPC on the special parts of the 2010 Statute. The final answer will probably be given in it. Everything pleads in favour of the rejection of the alternativity.

3 Conclusion

In conclusion, the exception mechanisms are also part of the determination of the applicable law.

Public policy and overriding mandatory provisions can be found in both systems.[36] But we are not gone to study them in detail for a good reason. They have no real impact on the international sale of goods contracts between Europe and China. There is no real example of a concrete application by the judges of such mechanisms in our field.

Sale of goods contract will only be indirectly concerned. The best example can be found in the Chinese system. Article 10 of the 2012 Supreme Court's Interpretation gives a non-exhaustive list of fields in which the mechanism of overriding

---

[35]For the same opinion, He (2012), p. 64.

[36]For public policy, **article 21 of the regulation Rome I**: "*The application of a provision of the law of any country specified by this Regulation may be refused only if such application is manifestly incompatible with the public policy (ordre public) of the forum*" and **article 5 of the Statute** "*Where the application of a foreign law will be prejudicial to the social and public interest of the PRC, the PRC law shall be applied*". For overriding mandatory provisions, **Article 4 of the Statute** "*Where a mandatory provision of the law of the People's Republic of China ('PRC') exists with respect to a foreign-related civil relation, that mandatory provision shall be applied directly*" and **Article 9 of the Regulation Rome I**: "1. *Overriding mandatory provisions are provisions the respect for which is regarded as crucial by a country for safeguarding its public interests, such as its political, social or economic organisation, to such an extent that they are applicable to any situation falling within their scope, irrespective of the law otherwise applicable to the contract under this Regulation.*

2. Nothing in this Regulation shall restrict the application of the overriding mandatory provisions of the law of the forum.

3. Effect may be given to the overriding mandatory provisions of the law of the country where the obligations arising out of the contract have to be or have been performed, in so far as those overriding mandatory provisions render the performance of the contract unlawful. In considering whether to give effect to those provisions, regard shall be had to their nature and purpose and to the consequences of their application or non-application".

mandatory provisions can be used. Sale of goods cannot be found in itself in that list. But a provision concerning safety of food, a critical issue in China, can be considered as directly applicable. This means that a contract between a French and a Chinese firm about the sale of food, which is a kind of goods, can be affected by such a Chinese provision, which will be applied if a Chinese judge knows of the case. The application by a European judge of such a Chinese rule could also be imagined, according to article 9 § 3 of Rome I Regulation, which concerns the foreign overriding mandatory provisions. However, this article has never been used yet.[37]

Of course, in the Member States of the European Union, this mechanism can also be used to apply national provisions. The best examples can be found about the protection of the consumer and are developed in another part of the book.[38]

References

Curti-Gialdino A (1972) La volonté des parties en droit international privé. Collect Courses Hague Acad Int Law 137:743–938

Cerqueira G, Nord N (2011) Comments on the chinese new statute on conflict of laws: a european perspective. Chin Yearb Private Int Law Comp Law 14:70–101

Deshayes O (dir.) (2012) Le droit commun européen de la vente-Examen de la proposition de Règlement du 11 octobre 2011. SLC, coll. TEE, Paris

Gaudemet-Tallon H JurisClasseur Droit international, Fasc. 552-11: Convention de Rome du 19 juin 1980 et Règlement "Rome I" du 17 juin 2008a. – Champ d'application. – Clauses générales

Gaudemet-Tallon H JurisClasseur Droit international, Fasc. 552-15, "Convention de Rome du 19 juin 1980 et Règlement "Rome I" du 17 juin 2008b – Détermination de la loi applicable. – Domaine de la loi applicable"

Guiliano M (1977) La loi applicable aux contrats: problèmes choisis. Collect Courses Hague Acad Int Law 158:183–270

Giuliano M, Lagarde P (1980) Report on the Convention on the law applicable to contractual obligations. Off J Eur Communities C 282:1–50

He Q (2012) The EU conflict of Laws communitarization and the modernization of chinese private international law. RabelsZ 76:47–85

Huang J, Du H (2005) Chinese judicial practice in private international law 2002. Chin J Int Law 4 (2):647–676

Huang J, Jiang R (2011) Zhonghua renmin gongheguo shewai minshi guanxi falü shiyong fa fanyi yu fenxi. Falv chubanshe, Beijing

Huo Z (2013) Two steps forward, one step back: a commentary on the judicial interpretation on the private international law act of China. Hong Kong Law J 43:685–712

Jacquet J-M Rép. Dalloz, Droit International, V°Contrats

---

[37] For a situation in which a foreign overriding mandatory has been taken into consideration but not applied, concerning the Rome Convention, a decision of the French *Cour de cassation*, Com. 16 March 2010, JCP 2010, 530, obs. D. Bureau and L. d'Avout and the decision in the same case of the Court of Appeal of Poitiers, 29 November 2011, RTD Com. 2012, 217, obs. P. Delebecque.

[38] See Chapter IV, Section II, "The law applicable to the Consumer contracts: protection and gaps in China and in Europe".

Lagarde P (1991) Le nouveau droit international privé des contrats après l'entrée en vigueur de la Convention de Rome du 19 juin 1980. Rev. crit. DIP: 287–340
Leibküchler P (2013) Erste interpretation des OVG zum gesetz über das internationale privatrecht. ZchinR 20:88–98
Li-Kotovtchikine X-Y (2002) Le nouveau droit chinois des contrats internationaux. Journal du droit International 129:113–163
Li-Kotovtchikhine X-Y (2010) Pragmatisme juridique et développement économique dans la chine post-Mao. Revue internationale de droit comparé 62(4):931–952
Mellone M, Nord N (2013) The influence of the European Union private international law on the new chinese conflict of laws statute. PKU Int Comp Law Rev 10:141–182
Pissler K (2012) Das neue Internationale Privatrecht der Volksrepublik China: Nach den Steinen tastend den Fluss überqueren. RabelsZ 76:1–46
Schulze R (ed) (2012) Common european sales law (CESL) – commentary. Beck, Hart, Nomos, Baden-Baden
Tu G, Xu M (2011) Contractual conflicts in the People's Republic of China: the applicable law in the absence of choice. J Private Int Law 7:179–202
Wang H (2009) A review of China's private international law during the 30-year period of reform and opening-up. ASLI Working Paper Series, WPS002, https://law.nus.edu.sg/asli/working_paper_d.aspx?sno=WPS002
Xiao Y, Long W (2009) Contractual party autonomy in chinese private international law. Yearb Private Int Law 193:193–209
Xu G (1989) Contract in chinese private international law. Int Comp Law Q 38(3):48–653
Zhang M (2006) Choice of law in contracts: a chinese approach. Northwest J Int Law Bus 26 (2):289–333

Part II
Arbitration, an Alternative Way

International Sale of Goods: Combination of Arbitration and Mediation in China

Song Lianbin

Mediation is one of the most precious estates of Chinese traditional culture. In some authors' opinions, the "non-action" (wu song), "non-litigation" (fei song), and "humble lawsuit" (jian song) ideas of Confucianism are similar to the ADR idea.[1] There are not much things involving laws and actions in Confucianism (for example, 听讼,吾犹人也,必也使无讼乎); the interpretations of those sentences are also different. In my opinion, the "non-action" theory is too ideal; the existence of a society in which there is no dispute is not possible. Confucianism only encourages people to "review themselves three times a day" to avoid conflict but not to try to solve the problems by lawsuit; it suppresses judicial action, and it can only be considered as a halfway ADR. Some authors consider that the "non-action" theory has obstructed the development of the rule of law.[2]

At present, China International Economic and Trade Arbitration Commission (CIETAC) encourages the combination of arbitration and mediation, which has been accepted and developed by other Chinese arbitration commissions established after the Arbitration Law of 1994 entered into force and which has also affected other countries. According to Mr. TANG Houzhi, a founding member of CIETAC, although there was no provision about mediation in its early rules, CIETAC has combined mediation with arbitration in practice from the very beginning. The arbitrators started the arbitration process only if mediation was impossible.

Lately, mediation is getting more and more attention from the legislator and the Supreme People's Court. From 2000, there have been six important laws, as well as judicial interpretations and administrative regulations, on mediation. Some examples are "Law of Mediation and Arbitration of Labor Disputes" of 2008,

[1]Martin Odams De Zylva (2000), p. 15.

[2]Xiahong (2006), p. 124.

S. Lianbin (✉)
Faculty of International Law, Chinese University of Political Science and Law, Beijing, China
e-mail: songlianbin@aliyun.com

N. Nord, G. Cerqueira (eds.), *International Sale of Goods*, China-EU Law Series 5,
DOI 10.1007/978-3-319-54036-8_4

"Provisions on several issues concerning civil mediation work in People's Courts" of Supreme People's Court of 2004 (fa shi 2004 N 12), "several provisions on People's mediation work" of the judiciary ministry of 2002. Also, there are 17 laws and judicial interpretations that involve mediation, for example, "Interpretation I on several issues about application of Marriage Law."[3]

In China, mediation exists not only in judicial trial procedure but also in arbitration. As a matter of fact, Chinese laws and legal practice encourage the combination of arbitration and mediation.[4] I would like to introduce this special system—its definition (Sect. 1), its advantages and defects (Sect. 2), and its justifiability (Sect. 3)—and conclude with some of my advice on how it could be made better (Sect. 4).

1 Definition and Classification

The combination of arbitration and mediation, which are two dispute resolutions independent from each other, is a compound resolution of disputes. In Chinese legal practice, this system is mainly manifested as mediation proceeding during arbitration. It is also called combination of arbitration and mediation in a narrow sense. The parties submit their disputes to arbitration, and during arbitration, the arbitrator(s) tries (try) to engage in mediation. The mediation either succeeds or results to nothing, and they return to arbitration. On the other hand, combination of arbitration and mediation in a large sense means mediation before arbitration, arbitration in parallel with mediation and conciliation of the parties during the arbitration, etc.

In practice, there are three kinds of combination of arbitration and mediation: the first one is called "face to face," which means the arbitrator and both parties discuss together the issue; the second one is called "back to back," which means the arbitrator negotiates separately with each of the parties; the last one is mediation in supervise, which means without the arbitrator, the parties negotiate with each other on their own within the time limit given by the arbitral tribunal.[5]

As for the combination of arbitration and mediation in a large sense, it is a compound of arbitration and mediation in many ways.[6] The following models are the most classic.

The first one is "med-arb," which means the parties proceed to mediation procedure before the arbitral procedure. Normally, the mediator is not the arbitrator. The Arbitration Commission of Beijing made the "Mediation rules" in 2007, which was modified in 2011, according to which it applies the "med-arb" model.

[3]Fa shi 2001, n°30.

[4]Houzhi (2002), p. 50.

[5]Ming (2007), p. 92.

[6]Shengchang (2001).

The second one is arbitration in parallel with mediation, which can be divided into two kinds: shadow mediation and co-med-arb. In shadow mediation, the parties begin with arbitration, during which they engage in parallel mediation. In this type of mediation, the mediator and the arbitrator are different. The mediation and arbitration may even be held in two different institutions. In co-med-arb, the arbitrator and mediator are also different. They attend the public hearing together, but the arbitrator does not attend the private meeting between the mediator and the parties. The mediator will disclose confidential information that he has obtained during the mediation to the arbitrator. In the next phase of the arbitration, the arbitrator may try to mediate when he thinks the time is right.

The third one is med-post-arb, wherein after the closure of arbitration, the parties will try to solve the issues that arose during the execution of the arbitral award by mediation. In some special cases, the parties may consent to a settlement in the execution phase of arbitration.[7]

2 Advantages and Defects

Lately, the combination of arbitration and mediation has been accepted by more and more practicians because of its advantage of saving time and efficiency. However, it is also questioned for some defects.

2.1 Advantages

Firstly, the combination of mediation and arbitration respects the parties' autonomy and makes resolution more flexible. During the last few years, more and more "potential parties" censure the arbitration for "litigationize." The complexity and lengthiness of arbitral procedure and the "circle" of the arbitrator candidates are weakening the traditional advantages of arbitration such as efficiency, saving of time, simplicity, and neutralization. The combination of arbitration and mediation can lessen the cost of parties with respect to time, money, and attention and can lead quickly to the resolution of their disputes so that they can return to their normal businesses as soon as possible.

Secondly, it can relieve the courts from the burden of judicial control and execution. If the parties settle for reconciliation during the arbitration procedure, they can request the arbitral tribunal to render an award based on their settlement, in order for it to be covered by compulsory enforcement. The concerned award, which was made completely based on the parties' autonomy, is more likely performed voluntarily by the parties.

[7]Guicai (2001), pp. 51–52.

Thirdly, it is better for maintaining the relationship between the parties. The respect of the parties' autonomy is the common characteristic of arbitration and mediation. The combination of the two is no doubt a double guarantee. It is easier for the parties to continue their business cooperation in the future.

Finally, it can improve the efficiency of resolution of disputes. The combination of arbitration and mediation can save the time for an independent mediation procedure. Even if the mediation has not succeeded, the arbitrator is already familiar with the case, so he can solve the dispute more quickly when they return to arbitration.

2.2 *Defects*

Although the combination of arbitration and mediation has the above-mentioned advantages, some authors have pointed out its defects. They are mainly three.

The first one is doubt with respect to natural justice and due process. According to the mediation system, the mediator can communicate with the parties by "alternate secret talks" and "shuttle diplomacy." However, both of these techniques conflict with the impartiality of arbitration. For example, the mediator has acknowledged the opinions of one of the parties by secret talks, but the other party is aware of nothing, so he loses the opportunity of arguing about it. This situation may cause the mediator to make false effort for the resolution. So this "back-to-back" technique, which is based on the good faith of the parties, requires a high-level qualification of the mediator himself.

The second one is the confusion caused by the coincidence of the identities of the arbitrator and mediator. The information gathered by the arbitrator during the mediation procedure may affect the arbitral award because the arbitrator is also a perceptual person, which makes him sometimes difficult to make a distinction between the information gathered during the mediation and the parties' opinions presented during the arbitration. So the arbitrator may render the arbitral award based on the parties' opinions presented during the mediation procedure.

The third one is that the combination of arbitration and mediation may cost more time and money and may lessen the efficiency of arbitration. In the arbitration held in Mainland China, the arbitral tribunal usually encourages the parties to conciliate in order to maintain their business relationship. However, if they spend too much time and attention to mediation, which may result to nothing, the procedure of arbitration will be slowed down, which makes the parties throw doubt upon the combination of arbitration and mediation.

3 Justifiability

Based on the above-mentioned analysis, the international arbitration community has two different attitudes concerning the combination of arbitration and mediation.

For commercial operation considerations, some judges and authors[8] think that regardless of the result, the combination of arbitration and mediation can save some unnecessary costs and accelerate the resolution of disputes. If the mediation achieves success, the parties and the arbitral tribunal can save plenty of time and money. If the mediation fails, they will be aware of the central point of the dispute, and that makes the next procedure more efficient. These favorable positions can be enumerated as follows: the wealth theory, benefit theory, responsibility theory, trust theory, and progress theory.[9]

As for arbitral practitioners, arbitration and mediation are two procedures fully consistent with the due process principle. The two parallel dispute resolution mechanisms should not be confounded. So the oppositional ones have pointed out the encroachment theory, the confusion theory, the incontrollable theory, and the risk theory.

Most of Chinese arbitral practitioners are in favor of the combination of arbitration and mediation. We think that the "private visit" of the arbitrator to one of the parties does not harm the due process of arbitration and the professional capacity of the arbitrators, and the mediators can avoid the influence of the parties' opinions on their neutrality and objectivity.

4 Advice

The core of alternative dispute resolution mechanism is pluralism and flexibility. It means that the parties have more independent resolutions for their disputes, so that may reduce the frequency of use of public jurisdiction resources. Theoretically, in civil and commercial matters, if the parties have equal sense and acknowledge the resolution of their disputes, no doubt arbitration becomes more efficient than a lawsuit. But with the arbitration becoming more and more like a litigation, it requires more and more the participation of lawyers and confrontation procedure. So the advantages of arbitration slightly disappear. In my opinion, although the combination of arbitration and mediation can remedy it in some way, it is not good enough compared to independent mediation. Even though arbitral mediation is executable in law, the reconciliation agreement cannot be the basis of compulsory enforcement by the courts. From this point of view, the Beijing Arbitration Commission has paid attention to both the value of mediation and the executable result by establishing a special Mediation Rules. I would like to offer three pieces of

[8]Schmitthoff C. M., translated by Xiuwen (1993), pp. 648–649.

[9]Shengchang (2001).

advice based on my work experiences gained from CIETAC and the Beijing Arbitration Commission.

First of all, we should focus on respect of the parties' autonomy. The common accord of the parties is the initial basis of the mediation. The respect of the parties' autonomy would avoid the aggravation of conflict of the parties' interests, lead the parties to the way of self-resolution, and thus achieve harmonization between them. For example, different from the withdrawal of arbitrators in arbitration, the mediator must try his best to earn the approval of the parties.

Second, there must be a "no-prejudice to the *status quo*" clause. To encourage the mediation, the clause is included usually in the arbitration rules and mediation rules, which means that if the mediation fails, any of the parties cannot use the statements, opinions, advice, or documents gathered during the mediation as the basis of their request, reply, or counterclaim in the next arbitral or judicial procedure. The parties cannot request the mediator to be a witness in the above-mentioned procedures. But we should notice that only the documents and information gathered during the mediation that cannot be used in subsequent procedures and not all that have been obtained during the mediation.

Third, if the mediation fails, the parties can ask to change the arbitrator. If the mediation does not work, it may affect the judgment of the arbitrator. So allowing the replacement of the arbitrator or requesting that the mediator cannot be the arbitrator is practicable in some way. For example, in a CIETAC case that concerns the international sale of goods, the arbitral tribunal learned that the concerned goods are suspected of being smuggled. After the mediation failed, the arbitral tribunal declined its competence on the case considering the legality of the sale. Objectively, the mediation does affect the arbitral tribunal in some way.

5 Conclusion

As one of the most classic ADRs, mediation has a long history in China. The Chinese arbitration commissions apply usually the combination of arbitration and mediation. But it is just a versatility of arbitration. Only the independent mediation administered by the arbitration commission is the real professional mediation. Although the success of mediation depends more on the acknowledgment, intelligence, communication technique, and persuasive skills of the mediator, the development of judicial environment is not dispensable. If we focus on the influence of the parties to the result, it can be said that being an arbitrator is harder than a judge and being a mediator is even harder than an arbitrator. And among the mediators, the mediator in combination of arbitration and mediation in a narrow sense requires more acknowledgment, experience, and skills than the mediators of combination of arbitration and mediation in a large sense.

References

Guicai H (2001) Solution to difficult execution of CIETAC award in HK and He Bei by mediation. China Arbitr 2:51–52
Houzhi T (2002) Expending culture: combination of arbitration and mediation or ADR. China's Foreign Trade 2:50
Ming K (2007) Several issues about the combination of arbitration and mediation. Beijing Arbitr Q 61:92
Schmitthoff CM translated by Xiuwen Z (1993) Select Essays on International Trade Law, ECPH
Shengchang W (2001) Study of the system of combination of arbitration and mediation. Univ Int Bus Econ
Xiahong C (2006) Profiles of Chinese legal persons in centuries. China Legal Publishing House, Beijing
Zylva MOD (ed) (2000) International commercial arbitration:developing rules for the new millennium. Jordan Publishing Limited, Bristol

Arbitration in the Field of International Sale of Goods: A French Point of View

Jochen Bauerreis

In the morning, my colleagues have elaborated the European and Chinese solutions regarding the identification of the judge and the applicable law in the field of international sale of goods.

In the afternoon, we concentrate on more unconventional approaches, such as arbitration.

My colleague has just analysed the relationship between the international sale of goods and arbitration in China, and I will elaborate the particularities regarding this subject in Europe and especially in France.

We will first study the place of arbitration within the alternative dispute resolution system (Sect. 1). Then we will concentrate on France and the important reform of 2011 that changed part of the arbitration procedure (Sect. 2). After having given a framework of the arbitration system in France, we will demonstrate the affinity between the CISG and arbitration by giving practical examples (Sect. 3).

1 International Arbitration Within the ADR System

After having given a definition of arbitration and the arbitrability of a dispute (Sect. 1.1), we will talk about the classifications of arbitration (Sect. 1.2) and its advantages and disadvantages (Sect. 1.3).

J. Bauerreis (✉)
Faculty of Law, University of Strasbourg, Strasbourg, France
e-mail: jochen.bauerreis@unistra.fr

N. Nord, G. Cerqueira (eds.), *International Sale of Goods*, China-EU Law Series 5,
DOI 10.1007/978-3-319-54036-8_5

1.1 Definition of Arbitration and the Arbitrability of a Dispute

While defining what arbitration is, we shall, on the one hand, distinguish arbitration from mediation (Sect. 1.1.1) and, on the other hand, determine the scope of arbitration as an alternative dispute resolution method, which raises the question of whether all disputes are arbitrable (Sect. 1.1.2).

1.1.1 Arbitration vs. Mediation

Alternative dispute resolution refers to procedures for settling disputes by means other than litigation before national courts,[1] the most established and frequently used being arbitration and mediation. These techniques are not mutually exclusive; on the contrary, mediation is often attempted before arbitration, and the latter is applied as a procedure of last resort.[2]

While mediation is the attempt to settle a legal dispute through the active participation of a third party, the mediator, who works in order to help parties reach a conclusive and mutually satisfactory agreement,[3] arbitration consists in the submission of the dispute to one or more arbitrators and the proceedings usually end with a decision called an 'award', which has essentially the same value as an ordinary judicial judgment.[4]

1.1.2 Arbitrability of a Dispute

Parties can submit their dispute to arbitration either by introducing an arbitration clause in their initial contract or by concluding an arbitration agreement once a dispute arises.[5] Arbitration is mostly used for disputes resulting from legal relationships dealing with international commerce and therefore undoubtedly also for CISG-governed transactions. However, not all disputes can be submitted to arbitration. In fact, the subject matter must be arbitrable.

International conventions have not directly laid out the requirements for arbitrability; therefore, the determination of whether a dispute is arbitrable or not has been left to the national legislation of each State.[6]

---

[1] Joly-Hurard (2013), n°1; Foulon and Strickler (2014, actualisation: May 2016), n°1 and following.

[2] Moreau (2012), n°37 and 41–42.

[3] Joly-Hurard (2013), n°17.

[4] Loquin (2013), n°1–3; Moreau (2012), n°1.

[5] Loquin (2015), n°46; Loquin (2014), n°1.

[6] Loquin (2016), n°1–2; Loquin (2015), n°75.

1.1.2.1 France

In France, the legislation distinguishes between domestic and international arbitration.

In the field of domestic arbitration, a dispute is arbitrable when the matter concerns 'disposable rights', which excludes, according to article 2060 of the French Civil Code, not only matters of an individual's status and capacity but also public-policy-related matters.[7]

In the field of international arbitration, however, almost all disputes are arbitrable. The reason for the ample arbitrability in international arbitration is that the arbitration agreement is generally considered as being valid and therefore the dispute must be considered as being arbitrable. The grounds for inarbitrability are thus exceptional and limited to international public policy issues such as 'asset matters' related, for example, to insolvency law, intellectual property and competition law.[8] However, a dispute is not automatically considered as being inarbitrable solely because public policy rules apply. These rules can directly be applied to the merits of the dispute by the arbitral tribunal.

1.1.2.2 Other Legal Systems

Other legal systems use more concrete criteria in determining whether a dispute can be settled by arbitration. Swiss law, for example, provides that any claim involving an economic interest can be the subject of an arbitration agreement (article 177 (1) of the Federal Statute on Private International Law),[9] and the US Federal Arbitration Act of 1925[10] and the case law resulting from its application provide that any matter that does not concern a significant federal interest expressed in a federal law can be subject to arbitration.

1.2 Classifications of Arbitration

The main types of arbitration are, on the one hand, international and domestic arbitration (Sect. 1.2.1) and, on the other hand, (Sect. 1.2.2) institutional and *ad hoc* arbitration.

---

[7]Moreau (2012), n°88–96.

[8]Hascher (2005), n°22–32; Moreau et al. (2016), n°312–321.

[9]Bundesgesetz über das internationale Privatrecht (IPRG): https://www.admin.ch/opc/de/classified-compilation/19870312/index.html.

[10]US Federal Arbitration Act of 1925: http://www.sccinstitute.com/media/37104/the-federal-arbitration-act-usa.pdf.

1.2.1 Domestic vs. International Arbitration

This classification is of importance because many legal systems apply two different sets of rules to domestic and international arbitration. We can observe in general that rules applying to international arbitration are less restrictive and are supposed to confer more individual freedom to both parties and arbitrators than those governing domestic matters.

How can we distinguish domestic from international arbitration? National or domestic arbitration deals purely with national or domestic matters. In other words, all the elements of the arbitration must be related to one jurisdiction. As for international arbitration, no uniform definition exists.[11] However, under the rules and practices of arbitration institutions, a dispute may be regarded as international in reference to its nature (*ratione materiae*) or its parties (*ratione personae*).

For example, the UNCITRAL model law combines these two approaches in its article 1 (3):

> An arbitration is international if:
>
> (a) the parties to an arbitration agreement have, at the time of the conclusion of that agreement, their places of business in different States; or
>
> (b) one of the following places is situated outside the State in which the parties have their places of business: (i) the place of arbitration if determined in, or pursuant to, the arbitration agreement; (ii) any place where a substantial part of the obligations of the commercial relationship is to be performed or the place with which the subject-matter of the dispute is most closely connected; or
>
> (c) the parties have expressly agreed that the subject matter of the arbitration agreement relates to more than one country.[12]

In French law, article 1504 of the Code of Civil Procedure states in a very wide drafted formulation that

> An arbitration is international when international trade interests are at stake.[13]

1.2.2 *Ad hoc* vs. Institutional Arbitration

When submitting a dispute to arbitration, the parties can choose between two systems, *ad hoc* (Sect. 1.2.2.1) and institutional arbitration (Sect. 1.2.2.2). Both systems must be compared in detail in order to identify the most important differences between them (Sect. 1.2.2.3).

---

[11] Moreau et al. (2016), n°2.

[12] UNCITRAL model law: https://www.uncitral.org/pdf/english/texts/arbitration/ml-arb/06-54671_Ebook.pdf.

[13] Bureau (2007), p. 455; Laazouzi (2011), p. 704.

1.2.2.1 *Ad hoc* Arbitration

Parties engaging in *ad hoc* arbitration are responsible for determining and agreeing on their own arbitration procedures rather than being supervised by an arbitral institution and being subject to its procedural rules.[14] The parties choose not only the location of the arbitration, the language of the arbitration, the law applied to the dispute and the number and identity of the arbitrators but also the arbitration administrative rules themselves.

In case parties cannot agree on the above-mentioned administrative modalities for setting up the procedure, they are in general entitled to seek assistance from national courts. However, in such a case, the national court will not act as a judge empowered to decide on the merits of the dispute but solely as a 'judge acting in support of the arbitration' (in French and Swiss laws also called *juge d'appui*), whose powers are imperatively limited to administration issues.[15]

1.2.2.2 Institutional Arbitration

The parties can also choose to designate an arbitral institution. Institutional arbitrations are conducted in accordance with pre-established formal procedures and rules designed to assist them. The chosen institution may administer the arbitration according to its own rules.[16] Therefore, the arbitral institution will provide the parties with the same kind of purely administrative services[17] that, in the case of *ad hoc* arbitration, the parties themselves, if necessary with the assistance of national courts ('judge acting in support of the arbitration'), are supposed to render.

The main arbitral institutions and arbitration courts are the International Chamber of Commerce (ICC), founded in 1923 and located in Paris; the American Arbitration Association/ICDR (AAA), founded in 1926; the Beijing Arbitration Commission (BAC), established in 1996; the China International Economic and Trade Arbitration Commission (CIETAC), founded in 1956; the Vienna International Arbitral Centre (VIAC), established in 1975; the Chamber of National and International Arbitration Milan (CAM), founded in 1985; the Australian Centre for International Commercial Arbitration (ACICA), founded in 1985; the Swiss Chambers Arbitration Institution, established in 2004.

[14] Moreau (2012), n°7.

[15] Moreau (2012), n°258–265.

[16] Loquin (2013), n°28.

[17] Moreau (2012), n°8.

1.2.2.3 Comparison Between Both Systems

Generally, in international matters, parties prefer opting for institutional and not *ad hoc* arbitration because the latter does not offer an organisation framework for conducting the arbitration proceedings. The lack of procedural rules and the absence of an institution administering the arbitration leave the parties often unsettled.

However, the parties shall not forget that *ad hoc* arbitration comes with several advantages related to an economical interest and to legal security.

First, *ad hoc* arbitration has an economical advantage. In fact, it is generally less expensive than institutional arbitration since the parties do not have to pay a commercial institution or court fees. Should they nevertheless have to pay some court fees, they are very low.

Second, *ad hoc* arbitration may also have a legal advantage. For example, under article 1454 of the French Code of Civil Procedure, 'any dispute relating to the constitution of an arbitral tribunal shall be resolved, if the parties cannot agree, by the person responsible for administering the arbitration or, where there is no such person, by the judge acting in support of the arbitration'. This means that in the case of an institutional arbitration, only the arbitral institution, as a private and commercial organism, will settle the controversy between the parties, whereas in an *ad hoc* arbitration the national judge acting in support of the arbitration will intervene and make a procedural decision. Therefore, the intervention of the arbitral institution is not final, as opposed to the decision made by the judge acting in support of the arbitration in the case of an *ad hoc* arbitration, since the risk that one party brings an action for annulment of the award before the national judges will persist.

1.3 Advantages and Disadvantages of Arbitration

When internationally acting companies prefer arbitration to classical litigation before national courts, they do so because of different advantages offered by arbitration (Sect. 1.3.1). Nevertheless, arbitration has also a number of disadvantages, even if we shall appreciate the legal effects of these supposed disadvantages very carefully (Sect. 1.3.2).

1.3.1 Advantages

In the context of international trade, arbitration is a very popular mean of dispute resolution. In fact, arbitration has several advantages. First, the parties can directly choose the arbitrator and ensure that he is an expert in the area of law regarding the dispute.[18] Second, arbitration procedures are time-wise efficient compared to

[18]Moreau et al. (2016), n°100–101.

classic procedures before national courts, which normally last much longer. Moreover, the procedural timetable, which is set by the arbitrator and the parties depending on their availability, is very flexible. In addition, arbitral proceedings can be made confidential.[19] Furthermore, the New York Convention of 1958,[20] which has been adopted by more than 150 States, has facilitated the enforceability of foreign arbitral awards at a global level. Lastly, arbitration is characterised by its neutrality, predictability and security.

1.3.2 Disadvantages

Even though there are several advantages of using arbitration, there are supposedly two main disadvantages regarding once more the aspects of economical interest (Sect. 1.3.2.1) and legal security (Sect. 1.3.2.2).

1.3.2.1 Economical Interest

There may be an economical disadvantage. In fact, arbitration is considered as being more expensive than proceedings before national courts.

However, if one compares the costs of arbitration and national court proceedings, it appears that at the beginning of the arbitration proceedings, the administrative expenses and the arbitrator's fees are quite high compared to national proceedings. Nevertheless, it must be taken into consideration that the total length of the judicial proceedings can be very long because there are several instances, which is not the case in arbitration, where there is only one instance. Furthermore, before national courts, there can be the need for translating drafted legal documents in the court's language, which can produce further costs.

All these potential costs have to be taken into consideration when comparing arbitration with national proceedings.

1.3.2.2 Legal Security

As for arbitration, we must recognise that there is a legal disadvantage regarding the problem of third party claimants, which are not parties to the arbitration agreement. In the case of a group of contracts, some parties may not be bound by an arbitration agreement while others are. Consequently, the problem can arise that an arbitral tribunal cannot include a third party in the proceedings, who has not given its consent, because it is not bound by the arbitration agreement.[21]

---

[19]Moreau et al. (2016), n°214.

[20]New York Convention of 1958: http://www.uncitral.org/uncitral/en/uncitral_texts/arbitration/NYConvention.html.

[21]Moreau et al. (2016), n°63–64.

The problem of third party claims can be resolved or attenuated in different ways. First of all, and from a theoretical point of view, the parties can of course insert the same arbitration clause in each individual contract, which is, however, in practice not very easy to achieve.[22] Alternatively, we can observe that national judges frequently intervene in favour of arbitration. In France, for instance, national judges are very favourable to arbitration. Therefore, the national courts often extend the individually concluded arbitration clause to the whole contractual grouping.[23] Finally, there may arise an evidentiary problem. Only parties to the arbitration are forced to follow the arbitral tribunal's orders. Third parties that possess evidence relevant to the dispute are not bound by the arbitration agreement and thus can only be ordered by French courts to produce such evidence, while national courts will only do so when the party requesting the measure has obtained the 'arbitral tribunal's invitation' to ask for the courts' assistance (article 1469 of the French Code of Civil Procedure).

2 Arbitration in France Since the 2011 Reform

Since 1981, France has adopted a very favourable law on arbitration granting parties great freedom. Thirty years later, the pro-arbitration approach of French law has been reinforced by decree no. 2011–2048 of 13 January 2011.[24] It changed the existing legislation governing arbitration by giving it more flexibility and reinforced the procedural powers conferred to arbitral tribunals. Furthermore, the reform has codified previous case law.[25]

First, we will identify the most important innovations of the 2011 arbitration reform (Sect. 2.1) and then reveal some of the most important differences between the French legislation regarding domestic and international arbitration (Sect. 2.2).

2.1 Important Innovations of the 2011 Arbitration Reform

Several major changes come with the 2011 arbitration reform, especially regarding the creation as a new legal concept of the judge acting in support of the arbitration (Sect. 2.1.1), the simplification of enforcement and review of arbitral awards (Sect. 2.1.2), the codification of jurisprudential principles (Sect. 2.1.3) and the abolishment of appeal of arbitral awards (Sect. 2.1.4).

---

[22] Moreau et al. (2016), n°65.

[23] Moreau et al. (2016), n°68.

[24] Hascher (2005), n°1.

[25] Bollée (2011), 553.

2.1.1 The Judge Acting in Support of the Arbitration

The decree of 2011 has created the judge acting in support of the arbitration (Sect. 2.1.1.1) and has defined the scope of his assistance regarding arbitration proceedings (Sect. 2.1.1.2).

2.1.1.1 The Role of the Judge Acting in Support of the Arbitration

First, the decree incorporates into French law the concept of the 'judge acting in support of the arbitration', the *juge d'appui*,[26] a concept originally borrowed from Swiss law and already known by the French doctrine and jurisprudence. The decree gives the judge acting in support of the arbitration, who is generally the President of the Paris' *Tribunal de Grande Instance*, the role to assist the parties in case they do not agree upon a certain matter, such as the constitution of the arbitral tribunal.[27]

2.1.1.2 The Scope of the Assistance of the Judge Acting in Support of the Arbitration

According to article 1452 of the French Code of Civil Procedure, the judge will only intervene on a subsidiary basis if the parties have not opted for an institutional arbitration.[28] If the parties have opted for the latter, only the institution itself has the authority to hear and decide on challenges brought against arbitrators. It must be pointed out that the judge is limited to giving assistance for merely administrative matters, for instance to appoint an arbitrator, and will not give any legal appreciation and make a decision on the dispute itself or the validity of the arbitration agreement.

The judge acting in support of the arbitration is meant to intervene when the parties have selected France as the place of the arbitration, French law as the applicable law to the arbitration procedure or French courts as having jurisdiction in the matter. Furthermore, he has a universal competence if one of the parties is exposed to the risk of a denial of justice, even if the dispute is not linked to the French legal order (article 1505 of the French Code of Civil Procedure).[29]

---

[26] Gaillard and De Lapasse (2011), p. 263, n°28–31.

[27] Bollée (2011), p. 553, n°7.

[28] Bollée (2011), p. 553, n 7.

[29] Gaillard and De Lapasse (2011), n°92.

2.1.2 Enforcement and Review of Arbitral Awards

Another innovation was introduced by the 2011 reform regarding the simplification of enforcement and review of arbitral awards in the field of international arbitration. In fact, according to article 1526 of the French Code of Civil Procedure 'neither an action to set aside an award nor an appeal against an enforcement order suspends enforcement of an award'.[30] Consequently, an award, which was rendered in France, will always be enforceable even if a party has filed an action to set aside the award.

In practice, the application of this rule, which does not apply to domestic arbitration, has a great impact: the losing party will not be able to file an action to set aside the award for the only purpose of delaying the award's enforcement.

2.1.3 Codification of Jurisprudential Principles

The 2011 arbitration reform has also asserted some important principles that have been established by the jurisprudence, such as

- the competence-competence principle;[31]
- the principle of procedural estoppel;[32]
- the principle of celerity;[33]
- the principle of independence and impartiality.[34]

2.1.4 The Abolishment of Appeal of Arbitral Awards

The reform of 2011 has entirely changed the legislation regarding the appeal of arbitral awards, in particular in international arbitration. In fact, according to article

---

[30]Bollée (2011), p. 553, n°25.

[31]The competence-competence principle has been defined by article 1465 of the French Code of Civil Procedure. According to this article "The Arbitral Tribunal has exclusive jurisdiction to rule on objections to its jurisdiction". In international arbitration, it is a general principle that the Arbitral Tribunal rules on its own jurisdiction.

[32]Article 1466 of the French Code of Civil Procedure defines the principle of estoppel: "A party which, knowingly and without a legitimate reason, fails to object to an irregularity before the arbitral tribunal in a timely manner shall be deemed to have waived its right to avail itself of such irregularity". According to this article, a party who has not objected to a procedural irregularity during the arbitration proceedings must not invoke this irregularity before a national court.

[33]The principle of celerity is implicitly affirmed in article 1464 paragraph 3 "Both parties and arbitrators shall act diligently and in good faith in the conduct of the proceedings". This provision aims at ensuring that the Arbitral Tribunal acts efficiently.

[34]According to article 1456 paragraph 2 of the French Code of Civil Procedure "Before accepting a mandate, an arbitrator shall disclose any circumstance that may affect his or her independence or impartiality". This means that the arbitrators have to disclose potential objections to the parties.

1518 of the French Code of Civil Procedure, the parties can only ask to set aside an arbitral award on limited grounds, such as the incompetence of the arbitral tribunal. The parties can no more appeal the arbitral award, which means that the award cannot be reviewed on the merits. In domestic arbitration, the award can still be subject to appeal, but only if the parties have agreed on that.

2.2 *Differences Between Domestic and International Arbitration*

France has maintained its dualist approach regarding domestic and international arbitration.

In general, international arbitration is less restrictive than domestic arbitration. The most important differences concern the validity of the arbitration agreement (Sect. 2.2.1), the confidentiality of arbitration proceedings (Sect. 2.2.2), the annulment of the arbitral award (Sect. 2.2.3) and the appeal of the arbitral award (Sect. 2.2.4).

2.2.1 The Validity of the Arbitration Agreement

Regarding the requirements of the validity of the arbitration agreement, French law governing domestic arbitration has defined the arbitration agreement, whereas the legislator has given no definition in the field of international arbitration. Moreover, only in domestic arbitration is the arbitration agreement required to be in writing;[35] the number of arbitrators must be uneven, and they cannot be legal entities.

2.2.2 The Confidentiality of the Arbitration Proceedings

An important distinction has been made regarding the confidentiality of the proceedings. According to article 1464 (4) of the French Code of Civil Procedure, arbitral proceedings shall be confidential. This article is applicable to domestic arbitration and has no equivalent in the chapter dedicated to international arbitration, which means that in case of the latter, the arbitral proceedings are not necessarily confidential.[36] The reason why this specific provision has been limited to domestic arbitration is because international public investment issues are often governed by transparency rules and therefore the arbitration proceeding should not be in general confidential. Nonetheless, the parties can of course expressly stipulate in the arbitration agreement that they wish the procedure to be confidential.

[35] Moreau et al. (2016), n°49.

[36] Moreau et al. (2016), n°216.

2.2.3 The Annulment of the Arbitral Award

In domestic and international arbitration, bringing an action for annulment of the arbitral award has not the same consequences. As stated above, in domestic arbitration, the action for annulment of the arbitral award has a suspensive effect on the latter, whereas in international arbitration it has no such effect. This means that in the field of international arbitration, the arbitral award is enforceable, even if an action for annulment is brought before a court.

2.2.4 The Appeal of the Arbitral Award

As mentioned above, in international arbitration, the parties can only set aside and not appeal an arbitral award, whereas in domestic arbitration, they can appeal an award if they have agreed upon it.

3 Practical Aspects of International Arbitration and the CISG

Even though international commercial arbitration and the CISG are two different legal instruments, there is a great deal of affinity between them. The one, an alternative mean of dispute resolution, and the other, a uniform international sales law, are both practice oriented and flexible. We would like to demonstrate in this third part that both legal instruments complement each other perfectly.

Therefore, we will first of all focus on the principle of party autonomy, which is a very important pillar in arbitration and the CISG (Sect. 3.1) and show how this principle is applied to practical aspects such as the battle of the forms and the possibility of opting in the CISG (Sect. 3.2).

3.1 The Principle of Party Autonomy

Party autonomy is an important pillar in the CISG and arbitration (Sect. 3.1.1) and is used by arbitrators as an interpretative standard to fill contractual gaps (Sect. 3.1.2).

3.1.1 Party Autonomy as an Important Pillar in the CISG and Arbitration

The autonomy of the parties is the most important pillar in both arbitration and the CISG.

3.1.1.1 CISG

In the CISG, article 6 guarantees the parties' autonomy by establishing that the parties can exclude the application of the CISG or modify any of its provisions.[37] Consequently, the parties have a great deal of freedom when deciding on what and how they would like the CISG rules to govern their contractual relationship.

3.1.1.2 Arbitration

The same goes for arbitration as an alternative dispute resolution method, which is exclusively based on the parties' will.[38] According to article 1511 of the French Code of Civil Procedure:

> Le tribunal arbitral tranche le litige conformément aux règles de droit que les parties ont choisies ou, à défaut, conformément à celles qu'il estime appropriées. Il tient compte, dans tous les cas, des usages du commerce.
>
> Translation:
>
> The arbitral tribunal shall decide the dispute in accordance with the rules of law chosen by the parties or, where no such choice has been made, in accordance with the rules of law it considers appropriate. In either case, the arbitral tribunal shall take trade usages into account.

3.1.2 Party Autonomy as an Interpretive Standard for Filling Contractual Gaps by Arbitrators

3.1.2.1 Filling of Contractual Gaps for Matters Not Governed by CISG (External Gaps in the Sense of Article 4) in the Absence of a Choice of Law

Article 4 CISG states that the Convention is not concerned with the validity of the contract, its provision or usage and the effect, which the contract would have on the property in the goods sold.[39] In this case, subsidiary national law applies, which

---

[37] Audit (2011), n°88.

[38] Loquin (2015), n°80.

[39] Audit (2011), n°82–84.

must, however, be interpreted in the light of the Convention. In the case parties have not expressly chosen a subsidiary national law, the question arises how the arbitral tribunal will determine the applicable law.

Article 1511 of the French Code of Civil Procedure focuses on party autonomy in a triple way.

First of all, article 1511 Code of Civil Procedure entitles the arbitrator in case the parties have not chosen the applicable law to their contractual relationship to apply the rules of law he considers 'appropriate'. Therefore, as a fundamental difference from national courts, arbitrators are not bound by the existing conflict rules as set forth, for example, in Rome I and II regulations.

This provision gives the arbitrator a great deal of flexibility. In fact, the flexibility results especially from the notion 'rules of law'. As opposed to statute law, this term has a much broader meaning and implies not only statutory but also soft law, such as *lex mercatoria* and/or the UNIDROIT principles.

Finally, the tribunal will always try to act in accordance with the explicit, implicit or presumed will of the parties. For instance, the arbitral tribunal can take trade usages into account when it esteems that its application was the implied will of the parties.

3.1.2.2 Filling of Contractual Gaps for Matters Governed by the CISG but Not expressly Settled (Internal Gaps in the Sense of Art. 7)

Article 7 CISG deals with the issue of (internal) gaps in the contract regarding matters governed by the Convention but not expressly settled by the latter. In this case, the gaps in the contract must be filled by referring to general principles of the Convention, and, only in the absence of these principles, national law must be applied.[40] These principles are not expressly set forth in the CISG but have to be deduced from the legal conception that has to be interpreted in the spirit of the CISG. Therefore, since arbitrators dispose of a larger margin of appreciation than national judges, we consider that arbitrators are probably in a better position to go, what the freedom of interpretation concerns, the whole way.

3.2 Practical Aspects of Party Autonomy

Two aspects can mainly illustrate the application of the principle of party autonomy: the battle of the forms (Sect. 3.2.1) and the possibility of opting in the CISG (Sect. 3.2.2).

[40] Audit (2011), n°103–104.

3.2.1 The Battle of the Forms

After having given a definition of 'battle of the forms' (Sect. 3.2.1.1), we will explain how the CISG provides for the application of the last-shot rule (Sect. 3.2.1.2) and how its application can be avoided (Sect. 3.2.1.3).

3.2.1.1 The Definition of 'Battle of the Forms'

In international transactions, the situation can arise in which the parties use standard form contracts containing conflicting general conditions. Each party will try to impose their general conditions in order to ensure their applicability. This situation can be defined as the 'battle of the forms'.

The legal framework of the CISG regarding the battle of the forms can be found under article 19.[41] The first paragraph of article 19 CISG is based on the mirror-image rule. According to this concept, in order to conclude a contract, an offer and an acceptance must correspond in all aspects. When the latter contains additions or alterations, it must be considered as a counter-offer and not an acceptance.

Article 19 (2) CISG tries to soften the severity of the mirror-image rule by allowing additional or different terms when the offeree's communication was intended to be an acceptance, the terms of the acceptance do not materially alter the terms of the offer and the offeror does not orally object to the altered terms.

3.2.1.2 The Last-Shot Rule as an Outdated Solution

It can be a very complex and difficult challenge for the courts to determine what the exact terms of the contract are. Both scholars and case law consider that article 19 (2) CISG incorporates the so-called last-shot rule. According to this rule, the terms contained in the last submitted form must be applied to the contract. The last-shot rule is based on the idea that if no valid objection has been made within a reasonable period of time, the party has tacitly accepted the terms. Consequently, the last person who sends its form is in control of the terms of the contract and wins the battle of the forms.[42]

This legal solution is not appropriate for modern and international business since it can give rise to legal insecurity. Therefore, in practice, this solution not only shall be criticised, but both parties and arbitrators should try to avoid it.

---

[41] Audit (2011), n°114.

[42] Mouly (1991), 77, n°2.

3.2.1.3 The Means to Avoid the Application of the Last-Shot Rule

The legal concept of the last-shot rule in the CISG is not only outdated but also incompatible with international commercial practice. Therefore, there are several ways to avoid the application of the last-shot rule. The parties can explicitly or implicitly exclude its application, or the exclusion of the rule can be presumed. First, according to the principle of party autonomy, the parties can expressly exclude the application of the last-shot rule under article 6 CISG. However, the problem can arise that parties fail to realise that the CISG is applicable to their contract. Consequently, they often do not provide for the exclusion of the last-shot rule because they are unaware of what rules the contract is subject to. Second, the parties can also implicitly waive the application of the last-shot rule. However, they must have a conclusive conduct.

When there is no explicit or implicit exclusion of the application of the last-shot rule, we can nonetheless presume that the parties wanted to exclude its application. In fact, we can consider that according to a widely spread business standard and/or trade usages, the parties would have preferred the last-shot rule not to be applied to the contract. The problem is that the last-shot rule comes with a procedural conflict, in particular for national judges. In fact, national judges are hesitant to presume the parties' will to exclude its application. Therefore, in case of doubt, they prefer following the safe path of what is exactly stipulated in the contract and applying the last-shot rule instead of the presumed will of the parties. In comparison with national judges, the arbitrator has much more flexibility and margin of appreciation, as we have already demonstrated above.

3.2.2 The Possibility of *Opting in* the CISG

The Convention automatically applies when all the legal conditions mentioned in article 1 and following are fulfilled.[43] Therefore, the parties do not need to 'opt in' the CISG, but they have the freedom to exclude the CISG according to article 6 (principle of 'opting out').

However, in case the legal requirements for the application of the CISG are not met, parties can nevertheless agree to opt in the CISG.[44] Such a contractual clause of opting in has a different scope when a dispute is brought before a national court (Sect. 3.2.2.1) or before an arbitral tribunal (Sect. 3.2.2.2).

[43] Audit (2011), n°73 and ff.

[44] Audit (2011), n°92–93.

3.2.2.1 Before a National Court

If brought before a national court, the clause will only have limited effectiveness. In fact, the CISG will not be applicable as the general law (*lex contractus)* of the international sale of goods because the contract is not within the scope of the CISG. Therefore, the national law of the State where the court has been seised will govern the contract. Only if the national law allows contractual derogations from the statutary provisions that are applicable will the national judge take the provisions of the CISG into account. Thus, the CISG will only be applicable if the national law leaves certain matters to the discretion of the parties. In this context, the CISG can be compared to 'soft law'.

3.2.2.2 Before an Arbitral Tribunal

The solution is different in arbitration. The arbitrator will give a great importance to the choice of law made by the parties. In comparison with the national court, which considers that the CISG is only a soft law, the arbitrator will consider it as being the *lex contractus*, in other words the substantive law of the contractual relationship. He will take national law only into account if the parties have stipulated that it must be applied as subsidiary law or to fill in gaps not covered by the provisions of the contract.

References

Audit B (September 2011, actualisation: June 2015) Répertoire Dalloz de Droit international: V°Vente Dalloz, Paris

Bollée S (2011) Le droit français de l'arbitrage international après le décret n° 2011-48 du 13 janvier 2011, Revue critique de droit international privé 2011:553

Bureau D (2007) Définition de l'arbitrage international et exclusion des voies de recours. Revue critique de droit international privé, Dalloz 2007:455

Foulon M, Strickler Y (February 2014, actualisation: May 2016) JurisClasseur Fasc. 1000: Modes alternatifs de résolution des litiges. – Conciliation – Procédure participative. Médiation. Lexis Nexis, Paris

Gaillard E, De Lapasse P (2011) Commentaire analytique du décret du 13 janvier 2011 portant réforme du droit français de l'arbitrage. Cahiers de l'arbitrage (Lextenso) 2:263

Hascher D (January 2005, actualisation: January 2016) Répertoire Dalloz de Droit international: Arbitrage du commerce international. Dalloz, Paris

Joly-Hurard J (March 2013, actualisation: June 2016) Répertoire Dalloz Procédure civile: Médiation et conciliation. Dalloz, Paris

Laazouzi M (2011) Définition de l'arbitrage international en fonction du dénouement économique de l'opération litigieuse. Revue critique de droit international privé (Dalloz) 2011:704

Loquin E (January 2013, actualisation: February 2015) JurisClasseur Procédure civile Fasc. 1005: Arbitrage. – Défintion. Nature juridique. Distinction avec d'autres institutions. Avantages et inconvénienrs. Lexis Nexis, Paris

Loquin E (July 2014, actualisation: October 2015) JurisClasseur Procédure civile Fasc. 1020: Arbitrage. – Compromis et clause compromissoire. Lexis Nexis, Paris

Loquin E (August 2015) JurisClassur Procédure civile Fasc. 1050: Arbitrage commercial international. - Notion. Lexis Nexis, Paris

Loquin E (May 2016) JurisClasseur Procédure civile Fasc. 1024: Arbitrage. – Conventions d'arbitrage. – Conditions de fond. Litige arbitrable. Lexis Nexis, Paris

Moreau B (December 2012, actualisation: April 2016) Répertoire Dalloz Procédure civile: Arbitrage en droit interne. Dalloz, Paris

Moreau B, Glucksmann E, Feng P (June 2016) Répertoire Dalloz de Procédure civile: Arbitrage international. Dalloz, Paris

Mouly C (1991) Que change la Convention de Vienne sur la vente internationale par rapport au droit français interne?, Recueil Dalloz (Dalloz) 1991:77

Integration of the Arbitral Award in the States System: Comparative Perspectives

Dong Jingjing

Traditionally, the enforcement of the arbitral awards relies on the voluntary performance of the parties as they have promised when they submitted their disputes to arbitration. According to a French author, about 90% ICC awards have been executed voluntarily.[1] However, the enforcement of the arbitral awards is not obligatory. In fact, the unfavorable party can challenge the concerned award before the courts. Meanwhile, the other party that wins can also go to a judge to apply for the compulsory enforcement of the arbitral award if the losing party does not perform it voluntarily. From then on, the arbitral award is no longer completely independent of the laws of the territory where the award is relied upon because the judge will use the laws to review the concerned award. Once the arbitral award is presented in front of a judge, it is subject to the national jurisdictions. Thus, it is very important to have knowledge of the laws of the territory where the arbitral awards are to be executed. After all, no one would like to take the risk that after spending all the money and time for the arbitration, an arbitral award cannot finally be enforced or even is set aside by the courts.

So I would like to talk about how the international arbitral awards integrate into the Chinese legal system and compare it with the French way and advise the European parties on the arbitration in China.

It is easy and hard to compare the Chinese and French laws in this field. It is easy because both systems have codified the rules for the judicial control of the arbitral awards, and some of them are quite similar. It is hard because not only the classification of the arbitral awards (Sect. 1) and the procedures of judicial control (Sect. 2) are different in two countries, but also the similar rules in the field of

[1]Cachard (2011), p. 538.

D. Jingjing (✉)
University of Strasbourg, Strasbourg, France

China University of Political Science and Law, Beijing, China
e-mail: 13811214822@163.com

N. Nord, G. Cerqueira (eds.), *International Sale of Goods*, China-EU Law Series 5,
DOI 10.1007/978-3-319-54036-8_6

recognition and enforcement of the international arbitral awards are interpreted differently (Sect. 3) in China and in France.

1 Classification of the Arbitral Awards

By comparing the Chinese and French laws, we can find that the classification of the arbitral awards is very different (Sect. 1.1), and the rules applicable to each one's recognition and enforcement are also very different (Sect. 1.2).

1.1 Different Classifications

Since the difference between the Chinese and the French classification of the arbitral awards is vast (Sect. 1.1.1), there are two advice for the European parties concerning the arbitration (Sect. 1.1.2).

1.1.1 Chinese and French Way of Classification

In French law, there are three sorts of arbitral awards: domestic arbitral awards, arbitral awards in matters of international arbitration, and the arbitral awards given abroad. The rules applicable for the recognition and enforcement of the last two sorts are so similar that they are codified in the same Chapter of *Code de procédure civile* (Chapter III: Recognition and enforcement in relation to arbitral award given abroad or in matters of international arbitration).

However, the Chinese law uses a different classification. There are also three sorts of arbitral awards: the domestic arbitral awards (article 58 of the Arbitration Law), the foreign-related arbitral awards rendered in China by the Chinese arbitral institutions (Chapter VII of the Arbitration Law: Special rules on foreign-related arbitration and article 271 of the Civil Procedure Law on setting aside of arbitral awards rendered by a Chinese foreign-related arbitration institution), and, the last sort, the arbitral awards rendered abroad by the foreign arbitral institutions (article 283 of the Civil Procedure Law on the recognition and enforcement of arbitral award rendered by a foreign arbitration institution).

1.1.2 Two Advice for European Parties

Because of these differences, there are two points that the European parties should pay attention before deciding the details about the arbitration.

The first one is that China still insists on institutional arbitration, which means that the *ad hoc* arbitral award rendered in China will not be recognized by any

Chinese jurisdiction even though the *ad hoc* arbitration is used very frequently to resolve commercial disputes. It is highly discouraged to choose *ad hoc* arbitration in China. As for the *ad hoc* arbitral award rendered abroad, it is safe. In 2015, the Supreme People's Court of PRC has published an judicial interpretation of the Civil Procedure Law, in which article 545 provides that for the recognition and enforcement of such award, the judges should apply the international treaties concluded or acceded to by China, so the UN Convention on the recognition and enforcement of foreign arbitral awards (the New York Convention of 1958), ratified by China in 1986, applies. And according to it, all arbitral awards, *ad hoc* or institutional, rendered in another Contracting State should be recognized and enforced in China, except for the cases provided by article V.

The second one is that neither the law nor the Supreme People's Court has indicated clearly the nature of the arbitral award rendered in China by a foreign arbitral institution. So the enforcement of this kind of awards may be obstructive. In the **Longlide vs. BP Agnati S.R. L case** of 25 Mars 2013, the parties have agreed that the dispute should be submitted to the ICC International Court of Arbitration, and the "place of jurisdiction shall be Shanghai, China." The Supreme People's Court decided that the agreement is valid.[2] In someone's opinion, this case shows the support of the Supreme People's Court for the foreign arbitration institutions processing arbitral actions in Mainland China.[3] However, the foreign arbitration institutions are still very prudent.

1.2 Different Applicable Laws

1.2.1 The French Solution

In France, the source is simple. There are national law (Sect. 1.2.1.1) and International Convention (Sect. 1.2.1.2) that rule the judicial control of the international arbitral awards.

1.2.1.1 The National Law

In France, as we have talked about before, both the arbitral awards rendered abroad and the international arbitral awards rendered in France are ruled by the *Code de procédure civile*, Book Four, Title II: International arbitration, which is amended by Decree N° 2011-48 of 13 January 2011. Chapter III is about their recognition and enforcement, in which article 1514 provides that "arbitral awards are recognized in France where the party who relies upon it has established their existence and if this

[2]Exiang W, the 4th Civil Chamber of the Supreme People's Court (2013), pp. 125–129.
[3]Ke and Xi (2015).

recognition is not manifestly contrary to public international order." Chapter IV is about the means of review, in which article 1520 provides five cases of setting aside an arbitral award given abroad or in matters of international arbitration. We should notice that only in these five circumstances could the French judges set aside the arbitral awards.

1.2.1.2 The International Convention

No doubt that it should be the national laws that should rule the recognition and enforcement of the international arbitral award rendered domestically. But when it concerns the recognition and enforcement of the foreign arbitral awards, it is usually the New York Convention of 1958 that applies. In the Convention, article V has provided seven cases in which the judge of a Contracting Country could refuse to recognize or enforce an arbitral award rendered in another Contracting Country. This Convention does help to guarantee the circulation of the arbitral awards among the countries, because more than 130 countries have ratified this Convention by now, including China and France.

Even though the New York Convention binds France, the French judges refer more to the French laws for the recognition and enforcement of foreign arbitral awards because according to article VII of the Convention, its application shall "not deprive any interested party of any right he may have to avail himself of an arbitral award in the manner and to the extent allowed by the law or the treaties of the country where such award is sought to be relied upon." Thus, since the French laws are looser than the New York Convention for the recognition and enforcement of foreign arbitral awards, the application of French laws, *Code de procédure civile* to be specific, is justified. The position of the French *Cour de Cassation* can be proved by the case of 29 June 2007.[4] In this case, the concerned award was rendered on April 10, 2001, in London by the International General Produce Association (IGPA). The French party has then requested for the *exequatur* of the award in France, and he had it. But the award was substituted by a new one on August 21, 2003, after a serial of actions before the English jurisdictions. So the Indian party appealed to the *Cour de Cassation*. But the judge of the *Cour de Cassation* upheld the decision of *Cour d'appel de Paris* explaining that according to article VII of the New York Convention, the French laws should apply and the award being set aside by the country where it was rendered is not a legal reason to refuse the recognition and enforcement of an international arbitral award.

[4]Cass. Civ. 1re 29 June 2007, n° 05-18.053, *Bull. civ.* I. n° 250.

1.2.2 The Chinese Solution

In China, the situation is much more complicated because it concerns so many relative laws, their juridical interpretations of the Supreme People's Court (Sect. 1.2.2.1), and the international treaties and arrangements (Sect. 1.2.2.2).

1.2.2.1 The Laws and the Juridical Interpretations

First of all, the Arbitration Law of 1994 rules generally the foreign-related arbitral awards rendered in China. Chapter V is about the review action of setting aside; Chapter VI provides the rules concerning compulsory enforcement, in which article 62 provides that the parties shall perform an arbitral award, and if one party fails to do so, "the other party may apply to a people's court for enforcement in accordance with the relevant provisions of the Civil Procedure Law, and the court shall enforce the award." Chapter VII provides some specific rules about foreign-related arbitration. Articles 70 and 71 concern the cases in which the court can decide to set aside and refuse the compulsory enforcement of a foreign-related arbitral award and they invoke directly article 260 clause 1 of the Civil Procedure Law, which became article 274 clause 1 of the Civil Procedure Law after an amendment in 2012. In 2006, the Supreme People's Court published the interpretation on the application of the Arbitration Law for practice details and supplies a gap in rules that the Arbitration Law fails to provide.

Second, both the Civil Procedure Law and the Supreme People's Court's interpretation have some specific rules for the foreign-related arbitral award rendered by the Chinese arbitral institution and the foreign arbitral awards. Article 274 of the Civil Procedure Law is one of the most important because it provides five cases in which the People's Court can refuse the enforcement and set aside the arbitral awards rendered by a Chinese foreign-related arbitral institution. Here we should explain three questions that may cause confusion for the European legal experts.

The first one is the usage of the term "foreign-related arbitral." In Chinese language, the meaning of "foreign-related" and "international" are quite similar. Both of them have two syllables, and both of them are composed of two characters. "Foreign-related" appears not only in the titles of some institutions but also in many legal documents. In the legislation history of PRC, since the "General Principles of Civil Law" of 1986, the Chinese legislature has always used "foreign-related" rather than "international." The Chinese codification of conflict of law of 2010 is also called "Law on the Application of Law to Foreign-related Civil Relations." In Interpretation I of the Supreme People's Court of the law, article 1 provides precisely five situations that should be determined to be foreign related.

The second one is why it mentions only the awards rendered by a foreign-related arbitral institution. We should notice that it does not mean that article 274 does not apply to the foreign-related awards rendered by other arbitral institutions. In 1956, the China Council for the promotion of International Trade (CCPIT) has established the first arbitral institution in China, the Foreign Trade Arbitration Commission (FTAC), the ancestor of the China International Economic and Trade Arbitration Commission (CIETAC).[5] It dealt specially and only with international commercial disputes between Chinese and foreign merchants. For decades, CIETAC has monopolized the "jurisdiction" over foreign-related cases, except international marine cases, which should be submitted to the China Maritime Arbitration Commission (CMAC). Between them and the other domestic arbitral institutions, there was a clear line, which was not erased until 1996 by a document of the general office of the State Department, in which article 3 provides that "the domestics arbitral institution can also accept the foreign-related cases if they are chosen voluntarily by the parties."[6] Article 274 (old article 260) of the Civil Procedure Law was created in 1991. At the time, these two foreign-related arbitral institutions rendered all foreign-related arbitral awards. So the expression was not wrong. But since the barrier was removed in 1996, the expression is no longer correct. Unfortunately, the Chinese legislature does not seem likely to correct this expression because there is no change in the following amendments of the Civil Procedure Law in 2007 and 2012. However, articles 70 and 71 of the Arbitration Law of 1994 clearly provide that if the parties prove that one of the situations provided by the article 260 clause 1 (present article 274 clause 1) of the Civil Procedure Law exists, the foreign-related arbitral award should be set aside (article 70) or its enforcement should be refused (article 71). We should pay attention to the fact that the Arbitration Law of 1994 used "foreign-related arbitral award," not "arbitral award rendered by a foreign-related arbitral institution." So there exists a tiny literal incoherence between the Arbitration Law and the Civil Procedure Law, but it does not affect the applicable law.

The last one is about the place where the foreign-related arbitral award is rendered. We should know that the Chinese arbitral institutions were not so international as they are now. In fact, all their awards were rendered in Mainland China until the CIETAC established the Hong Kong Arbitration Center in 2012. Since then, CIETAC has extended the place of arbitration to HK. We should notice that recently, an HK court has decided to accept a request for setting aside a CIETAC award rendered in HK. If the court approves it, that will be the first case in which a CIETAC award would be set aside outside Mainland China. We are still waiting for the following news.

1.2.2.2 The International Treaties

In 1986, China has ratified the New York Convention of 1958, and it came into force in 1987. According to the Convention, all arbitral awards, *ad hoc* or

---

[5]China International Economic and Trade Arbitration Commission (2015), http://www.cietac.org/index.php?m=Page&a=index&id=34&l=en. Accessed 24 Oct 2016.

[6]Chinese Government Public Information Online, http://govinfo.nlc.gov.cn/lssj/xxgb/nmgzb/19967/201104/t20110414_718090.html?classid=451. Accessed 24 Oct 2016.

institutional, rendered in another Contracting State should be recognized and enforced in China, except for the seven cases provided by article V.

For the arbitral awards rendered in the two special administrative regions, there are two arrangements of the Supreme People's Court on reciprocal enforcement of arbitral awards between Mainland China and HK (2000) and between Mainland China and Macao (2007).

For the arbitral awards rendered by a Taiwanese arbitral institution, the source is quite simple. In 1998, the Supreme People's Court has published "the provisions on recognition of civil judgments of Taiwan courts," and in 2009, the Supreme People's Court has published "the supplementary provisions," in which article 2 provides that the provisions of 1998 and the supplementary provisions of 2009 apply to the requests for recognition of arbitral awards rendered by a Taiwanese arbitral institution.

After comparing the applicable rules in China and in France, I would like to compare the procedures of the judicial control of the international arbitral awards.

2 The Procedures of Judicial Control of International Arbitral Awards

There are common things in general structure of the Chinese and French systems (Sect. 2.1), but these last are also quite different in details (Sect. 2.2). Chinese law presents therefore a specificity: the re-arbitation (Sect. 2.3).

2.1 The Convergence of the Procedures

2.1.1 The Recognition and Enforcement of the Foreign Arbitral Awards

In both systems, the recognition of the foreign arbitral awards does not equal their enforcement. In China, article 546 of the Judicial Interpretation of the Civil Procedure Law provides that the party requests to enforce the foreign arbitral award until getting the order of recognition. And if the party requests only to recognize the award, the court examines the concerned award and decides only whether to recognize it.

In France, the rules are the same. Articles 1514, 1523, and 1525 of *Code de procédure civile* use always the terms "recognized or enforced" or "recognition or enforcement."

2.1.2 The Enforcement Document

Article 1516 of *Code de procédure civile* provides that "the arbitral award may not be subjected to a compulsory enforcement by virtue of an *exequatur*." In China, according to article 240 of the Civil Procedure Law, the execution officer shall "send an enforcement notice to the person subjected to enforcement, and may conduct compulsory enforcement measures immediately."

2.2 The Divergence of the Procedures

2.2.1 The Recognition

According to article 1523 of *Code de procédure civile*, the French courts can recognize not only the arbitral awards rendered abroad but also the international arbitral awards rendered in France. But in China, only the awards rendered abroad need to be recognized (article 546 of the Judicial Interpretation of the Civil Procedure Law).

2.2.2 The Limitation of Action

There is no deadline for request to recognize or enforce the arbitral awards in French law, whether they were rendered in France or abroad. However, in Chinese law, according to article 239 of the Civil Procedure Law, the parties have only two years to apply for enforcement since the last day of the period of performance specified by the arbitral award, and without such period, since the day when the arbitral award has come into force. We should notice that before 2007, according to the old article 217 of the Civil Procedure Law of 1991, it was one year if both or one of the parties is a citizen and six months if both parties are legal persons or other organizations.

In French law, article 1519 of *Code de procédure civile* provides that the application for setting aside the arbitral award is admissible as soon as it has been rendered, but it will cease to be so if "it has not been brought within the month of the signification of the *exequatur*." In Chinese law, according to article 59 of the Arbitration Law, the review action to vacate should be initiated within six months since the day of receiving the arbitral award.

2.2.3 The Suspension of Enforcement

In French law, according to article 1526 of *Code de procédure civile*, neither the requests for setting aside an arbitral award nor the appeals of the exequatur order can suspend the procedure of enforcement. Only the chief president of the *Cour d'appel* or the "conseiller de la mise en état" can suspend the enforcement if it may seriously damage the rights of one of the parties.

However, article 64 of the Chinese Arbitration Law provides that if one party applies for enforcement while the other party requests to set aside the award, the People's Court shall decide to suspend the enforcement.

2.2.4 The Appeals and the Chinese Report System

In France, there is always a way to appeal. For the arbitral awards rendered abroad, the parties can appeal against the decisions of recognition and enforcement (article 1525 of *Code de procédure civile*). For the international arbitral awards rendered in France, the decisions disallowing the recognition or enforcement are subject to appeal (article 1523 of *Code de procédure civile*). Even the decisions of enforcement can be subject to appeal if the parties have already given up their rights of applying for setting aside the concerned award.

But in China, according to article 154 of the Civil Procedure Law, there is no way to appeal for any written order that sets aside or refuses to enforce the arbitral award, whether they were rendered in China or abroad. To explain that, we need to point out a special report system of Chinese law.

On August 28, 1995, the Supreme People's Court published a notice about the relevant matters of foreign-related and foreign arbitral awards. According to article 2, if the court decides to refuse the enforcement or recognition of a foreign-related arbitral award or a foreign arbitral award, it must report the decision to the High Court of its region for a review; the High Court, if it also agrees with the decision, must report the case to the Supreme People's Court. The decision that refuses the enforcement or recognition of the award cannot be made until the Supreme People's Court agrees with it in writing. Technically, the report system is a substitution of the appeal action system.

Obviously, there are some defects in this system. For example, it is administrative but not juridical. And there is no involvement of the parties. I would like to mention a big problem of this system in practice: there is no time limit for the Supreme People's Court to respond. The problem can be very obvious in an extreme case: on January 30, 1997, the Sugar Association of London rendered an arbitral award for a contract dispute that decided that a Chinese company should pay an American company 1,319,640 US dollars. In April 1997, the American company requested the recognition and enforcement of the award to the Intermediate Court of Nan Ning. In November 1998, the court decided to refuse the recognition of the award, so the American company reported to the High Court of Guang Xi. Then in November 2002, the Supreme People's Court returned the case to the Intermediate Court of Nan Ning for review. In June 2003, the court still decided to refuse to recognize the award. The case was reported to the High Court of Guang Xi and then to the Supreme People's Court again. Till February 2004, the Intermediate Court of Nan Ning decided to recognize and enforce the award. To enforce the award, the party waited for almost seven years.[7] Indeed, this case is a very regretful one, but it shows clearly the problem of the report system.

In my opinion, the report system is not a very efficient solution, but it is still necessary until the appeal system is established because without it, much more international and foreign arbitral awards may be refused to be enforced or even set aside by the judges of the Intermediate Courts and the High Courts by mistake, considering their limited knowledge on international private law.

2.3 *The Re-Arbitration*

Article 61 of the Chinese Arbitration Law provides that the court can return the case to the original arbitral tribunal to re-arbitrate within a time limit and suspend the procedure of setting aside an arbitral award. If the tribunal refuses, the court shall continue the setting aside procedure. Article 22 of the Judicial Interpretation of the Arbitration Law provides that if the arbitral tribunal begins the re-arbitration within the time limit, the court shall end the procedure of setting aside the arbitral award. According to article 23 of the Interpretation, the parties can still apply for setting aside the award within six months after the new one is rendered. As for the reasons of re-arbitration, it is still the four cases provided by article 274 § 1 of the Civil Procedure Law, which we will talk about in the next part.

3 Setting Aside or Refusal of Recognition or Enforcement of the International Arbitral Awards

In France, article 1520 of *Code de procédure civile* provides only five situations in which a judge may set aside an international arbitral award rendered in France (article 1520) or refuse the recognition or enforcement of an arbitral award rendered abroad (article 1525).

In China, articles 274 of the Civil Procedure Law also provides five cases of setting aside or refusing the enforcement of the international arbitral awards rendered in China. As for the foreign arbitral awards, and the awards rendered in HK and Macao, there are the New York Convention of 1958 and the arrangements of the Supreme People's Court, which provides the cases for refusing the recognition or enforcement. We should notice that the rules of the two arrangements are identical with article V of the New York Convention.

[7] Weiqi (2006), pp. 93–99.

3.1 The Competence of the Arbitral Tribunal and the Validity of the Arbitration Agreement

3.1.1 The Rules Applicable in Chinese Law and French Law

Article V § 1 clause a of the New York Convention provides that the recognition and enforcement of the award may be refused if "the arbitration agreement is not valid under the law to which the parties have subjected it."

In Chinese law, article 274 § 1 clause 1 provides the situation in which "the parties have not had an arbitral clause in the contract or have not subsequently reached a written arbitration agreement."

In French law, the old article1520 § 1 clause 1 of *Code de procédure civile* provided the situation in which "the arbitrator has ruled upon the matter without an arbitration agreement or based on a void and lapsed agreement." But in 2011, article 1520 was modified, and the new article 1520 § 1 clause 1 provided that "the arbitral tribunal falsely declares itself competent or incompetent."

Three of them are about the competence of the arbitral tribunal. The Chinese law and the New York Convention focus on the arbitration agreement, which is normally the basis for the competence of the tribunal. On the other hand, the present French rule is more general but not exhaustive. And it has included another situation that was not mentioned in the old article 274, which is that the arbitrator falsely declares himself incompetent.

We know that the validity of the agreement is very important to the competence of the arbitral tribunal, so it is very important to learn the national laws on determination of the validity of an arbitration agreement.

3.1.2 The Determination of the Validity of an Arbitration Agreement

The Chinese law is very different from the French law on this point.

3.1.2.1 The Rules Concerning the Validity of the Arbitration Agreement

According to articles 1507 and 1508 of the French *Code de procédure civile*, there is no formal condition for the agreement, so the parties have much more liberty to designate the arbitration institution. It can be written or verbal; the parties can designate an arbitration institution directly or by way of reference to its rules.

However, according to article 16 of the Chinese Arbitration Law, an arbitral clause and an arbitration agreement must be written and must contain three elements: the expression of the parties' wish to submit to arbitration, the matters to be arbitrated, and the arbitration commission selected by the parties.

Among the three elements, the third one, the selection of the arbitration commission, caused most problems in practice, which may cause the arbitration agreement to be null and void. So in the Judicial Interpretation of the Arbitration Law of 2006, the Supreme People's Court has pointed out some situations that should be considered when the parties have selected the arbitration commission. For example, "the name of the arbitration commission selected in the agreement is not correct but can still identify the arbitration commission" (article 3), "the parties have agreed on an arbitration commission of some place and there is only one arbitration commission in this place" (article 6).

But article 6 also provides that if there are two or more arbitration commissions in the place selected and the parties cannot agree on one of them, the agreement is null and void. So in the **Monarch vs. Haidi case**, of August 14, 2008, the Supreme People's Court decided that the arbitral clause "submit the dispute to the Arbitration Commission in Beijing" is null and void because there are two arbitration commissions in Beijing and the parties cannot agree on the selection of any of them.[8]

According to article 4, if the parties only point out rules of an arbitration commission, it should be considered that the parties have not agreed on the selection of the arbitration commission in the agreement. For example, in the **DMT S.A. vs. Dong Hong case** of January 12, 2006, the Supreme People's Court decided that the arbitral clause "ICC Rules, Beijing, shall apply" is null and void.[9]

And according to article 5, if the parties have agreed on two or more arbitration commissions in the agreement and cannot select together one of them, the agreement is null and void.

According to the decisions of the Supreme People's Court, the arbitral clause "submit the difference to the Arbitration Commission of the place where one (or any) party domiciles" is also problematic. In the **MCLANE case** of December 16, 2009, the Supreme People's Court agreed to set aside the Xia Men Arbitration Commission award <2008> Xia Zhong Cai Zi N°0379, because it is impossible to decide "one party" means which party and the "place of domicile" means the city or the province where the party domiciles.[10]

So in an arbitration agreement, it is better to indicate always the correct title of the arbitration institution selected by the parties.

As for the foreign arbitral awards that need to be recognized and enforced in China, we should notice that article II of the New York Convention provides that the Contracting State shall recognize the arbitration agreement only when it is "in writing." And article IV paragraph 1 provides that the party should supply the "original arbitration agreement referred to in article II or a duly certified copy thereof." Based on that, the Chinese courts have refused the recognition and enforcement of several foreign arbitral awards. In the **Hanjin Shipping Co., Ltd. vs. Fu Hong Oil Guang Dong case** of June 2, 2006, the Supreme People's Court has agreed to refuse the application for the enforcement of an *ad hoc* arbitral award rendered in London on December 6, 2004, for absence of arbitration agreement in

---

[8]Exiang W, the 4th Civil Chamber of the Supreme People's Court (2008), pp. 120–124.

[9]Exiang W, the 4th Civil Chamber of the Supreme People's Court (2006), pp. 103–104.

[10]Exiang W, the 4th Civil Chamber of the Supreme People's Court (2010), pp. 71–75.

writing.[11] And in the **Concordia Trading B.V. vs. Nantong Gangde case** of August 3, 2009, the Supreme People's Court agreed to refuse the recognition and enforcement of a FOSFA award explaining that the New York Convention does not accept a tacit arbitration agreement.[12]

3.1.2.2 The Competence to Determine the Competence of the Arbitral Tribunal

In French law, the competence-competence principle applies. So the arbitral tribunal decides by itself whether it is competent for the case. And if the tribunal considers itself competent, it can continue the procedure of arbitration and render the award.

However, according to article 20 of the Chinese Arbitration Law, not only the arbitration commission but also the courts could confirm the validity of the arbitration agreement. And if the parties apply simultaneously to the arbitration commission and a Court, the court shall give the ruling. If the court wants to declare a foreign-related arbitration agreement null and void, it should follow the report system, which means waiting until the Supreme People's Court responds.[13] And a response takes a really long time. The wasting of time is contrary to the original intention of the parties, who decide to resolve their dispute by arbitration.

3.2 The Procedural Matters

Clauses 2 and 3 of article 274 of the Chinese Civil Procedure Law concern the arbitral procedure. One is about the composition of the arbitral tribunal, and the other is about the notice for appointment of the arbitrator and the presence of the party against whom the award is invoked.

In French *Code de procédure civile*, article 1520 § 1 clauses 2 and 4 is similar but with some nuances. Article 1520 § 1 clause 4 only provides the case in which the adversarial principle has not been respected, but article 274 § 1 clause 2 provides that the party against whom the award is invoked was not given proper notice of the appointment of the arbitrator or of the arbitration proceedings or was unable to present his case due to cases for which he is not responsible. This rule is very similar to article V § 1 clause b of the New York Convention.

---

[11]Exiang W, the 4th Civil Chamber of the Supreme People's Court (2006), pp. 75–82.

[12]Exiang W, the 4th Civil Chamber of the Supreme People's Court (2009), pp. 75–86; Guixiang and Hongyu (2012), pp. 1–24.

[13]Article 2 of the "Notice of the Supreme People's Court to the people's courts concerning the questions relative to the treatment of the foreign-related and foreign arbitral cases", Fa Fa (1995) N°18, 28 August 1995.

3.3 The Scope of the Arbitration and Arbitrability

Article 1520 § 1 clause 3 of *Code de procédure civile* provides the situation in which "the arbitral tribunal has ruled upon the matter contrary to the assignment given to it." It is similar to article 274 § 1 clause 4 of the Chinese Civil Procedure Law and article V § 1 clause c of the New York Convention, except that the Chinese article 274 § 1 clause 4 has added another situation in which the arbitral institution was not empowered to arbitrate. So we should learn which type of cases cannot be settled by arbitration in Chinese law.

According to article 3 of the Chinese Arbitration Law, the disputes over marriage, adoption, guardianship, child maintenance, inheritance (paragraph 1, clause 1) and administrative disputes falling within the jurisdiction of the relevant administrative organs according to law (paragraph 1, clause 2) shall not be submitted to arbitration. The first cases are easy to understand, but sometimes it is difficult for the arbitral tribunal to decide whether the matters submitted to arbitration are administrative disputes falling within its jurisdiction or not. The Supreme People's Court has set aside several arbitral awards for this reason. And these cases may be enlightening.

In the **EA, RT vs. Jiangsu Huayuan Medicin case** of March 7, 2006, the Supreme People's Court decided that the CIETAC award has changed the proportion of the share stock authorized by the national vetting departments, which should be partly set aside.[14]

In the **Qingdao Jiacheng vs. VEM, SIMEST case** of April 22, 2011, the Supreme People's Court agreed to set aside a CIETAC award explaining that according to article 181 of the Chinese Company Law, an arbitration commission has no legal basis to disincorporate a company.[15]

3.4 The Social and Public Interest

According to article 1520 § 1 clause 5 of French *Code de procédure civile*, an arbitral award can be set aside if its recognition or enforcement is "contrary to the public international order," while article 274 § 2 of the Chinese Civil Procedure Law provides that the court may refuse the enforcement of or set aside an arbitral award if "it considers that the enforcement of the award is contrary to the social and public interest." The expressions are different, but the purposes are the same. But still, we should notice that the Chinese and French jurisdictions interpret and apply this rule in different ways.

---

[14] Exiang W, the 4th Civil Chamber of the Supreme People's Court (2006), pp. 90–95.

[15] Exiang W, the 4th Civil Chamber of the Supreme People's Court (2011), pp. 164–174.

3.4.1 The French Solution

We should notice that the French expression does not mean that there is such an international order. It is still about the French public interest. In French law, there is no definition of "violation of the public international order," but a series of French legal precedents shows that this exception exists for the "protection of fundamental laws." It must be "the recognition or enforcement of the award" not the award itself that violates the public international order, and the violation must be "flagrant, effective and concrete."[16]

3.4.2 The Chinese Solution

The Chinese judges refer to this rule more often than the French ones. Like in France, there is also no definition of "social and public interest" in Chinese law; the application of this rule depends on the interpretation of each judge himself.

There are not many arbitral awards rendered by the Chinese arbitration commissions that had been set aside or refused to be enforced for this reason. The most famous one is the **USA Productions, Tom Hulett & Associates vs. Chinese Woman Voyage case** of December 26, 1997, in which the Supreme People's Court decided that a CIETAC award concerning a conflict of a concert performance contract should not be enforced because the performance of heavy metal music had in fact violated the social public interest of PRC.[17] At the time, China was still a country not so open as she is now, so the situation is certainly changed now.

We should notice that article 274 § 2 of the Chinese Civil Procedure Law applies only to the foreign-related arbitral award rendered by the Chinese arbitral commissions; for the foreign arbitral awards rendered outside PRC, the judges apply the New York Convention. And article V § 2 clause b of the Convention provides that the recognition and enforcement of an arbitral award may be refused if the competent authority of a Contracting State finds that "the recognition or enforcement of the award would be contrary to the public policy of that country."

To foreign arbitral awards, the Chinese jurisdictions' position is more prudent. The Supreme People's Court has rejected lots and lots of requests coming from lower courts for refusing the recognition and enforcement of the foreign arbitral awards.

In the **Louis Dreyfus vs. Fuhong Oil case** of October 10, 2010, FOSFA has rendered an award in which the arbitrator said that there is a big distance between the laws and reality in China . . . the Chinese laws are very complicated . . . the most important is not how to interpret these rules but how to apply them in practice. The

---

[16] Cass. civ. 1re, 4 June 2008, n° 06-15.320, *Bull. civ.* I. n° 162; Cass. Civ. 1re 8 July 2010, n° 09-14.280, *Bull. civ.* I. n° 157; Cass. civ. 1re, 2 February 2014, n° 10-17.076, *Bull. civ.* I. n° 22.

[17] Exiang W, the 4th Civil Chamber of the Supreme People's Court (2009), pp. 226–227.

Supreme Court disapproved the request of refusing the recognition and enforcement of the award and considered that the misunderstanding of the Chinese law does not lead to a violation of the Chinese public interest.[18]

In the **Shin-Etsu Chemical Co., Ltd., vs. Zhongtian case** of June 29, 2010, after its award N°04-05 has been refused to be recognized in China, the Japan Commercial Arbitration Association (JCAA) rendered award N°07-11 to neutralize the damage; it even invoked the order of the Chinese court in the award. The Supreme People's Court disapproved that the recognition of the second award is a violation of the Chinese public policy because it doesn't violate the Chinese basic social interest.[19]

In the **Tianrui Hotel vs. Hangzhou Yiju case** of May 18, 2010, the London Court of International Arbitration (LCIA) rendered an arbitral award based on a franchise contract executed in China, which needs to be reported to the concerned administrative department for recording according to Chinese law. The Intermediate Court of Hangzhou and the High Court of Zhejiang wanted to refuse its recognition and enforcement for reason of fraud of law. But the Supreme People's Court disapproved the request explaining that the record system is administrative and does not affect the validity of the contract. The enforcement of the concerned award does not violate the Chinese social and public interest.[20]

Until now, the Supreme People's Court has approved to reject the enforcement of a foreign arbitral award for violation of the Chinese social and public interest only once, in the famous **Jinan Yongning Pharmaceutical case** of June 2, 2008. In this case, the Supreme Court declared that ICC has rendered an award over a contract dispute knowing that it has already been ruled by a Chinese court and that the Chinese court has ordered to impound the asset of the concerned company. The enforcement of the arbitral award will violate the Chinese judicial sovereignty and Chinese public interest.[21]

3.5 The Incapacity of Parties

Only the New York Convention makes the incapacity of parties a ground to refuse the recognition and enforcement of an arbitral award. We should notice that the Supreme People's Court has clarified for the first time, in the **Glencore case** of April 19, 2001, that the Chinese courts should apply Chinese law to review the capacity of the parties. In this case, Glencore applied for the recognition and enforcement in China of an arbitral award rendered by the London Metal Exchange. The Supreme Court refused the request explaining that agent Sun has neither been

[18]Exiang W, the 4th Civil Chamber of the Supreme People's Court (2011), pp. 181–188.
[19]Exiang W, the 4th Civil Chamber of the Supreme People's Court (2010), pp. 122–143.
[20]Exiang W, the 4th Civil Chamber of the Supreme People's Court (2011), pp. 175–180.
[21]Exiang W, the 4th Civil Chamber of the Supreme People's Court (2009), pp. 124–134.

authorized in the contract nor has sealed the contract. Therefore, his action does not represent Chongqing Machinery Import and Export Company.[22]

References

Cachard O (2011) International commercial law. LGDJ, Paris

Guixiang L, Hongyu S (2012) Review of the judicial practice of the recognition and enforcement of the foreign arbitral award in China. Beijing Arbitr Q 1:1–24

Ke H, Xi L (2015) Chinese law or no law? — About the procedural law on the arbitral actions of the foreign arbitration institution in Mainland China. Paper presented at the 8th Chinese arbitration and jurisdictions symposium, China Academy of Arbitration Law, Qingdao, 16 October 2015

Weiqi C (2006) Comments on a case of the "Marathon" judicial review of a foreign arbitral award. Arbitr Study 3:93–99

Cases

Cass. Civ. 1re 4 June 2008, n° 06-15.320, *Bull. civ.* I. n° 162

Cass. Civ. 1re 8 July 2010, n° 09-14.280, *Bull. civ.* I. n° 157

Cass. Civ. 1re 12 February 2014, n° 10-17.076, *Bull. civ.* I. n° 22

Chinese Government Public Information Online., http://govinfo.nlc.gov.cn/lssj/xxgb/nmgzb/19967/201104/t20110414_718090.html?classid=451. Accessed 24 Oct 2016

China International Economic and Trade Arbitration Commission (2015) http://www.cietac.org/index.php?m=Page&a=index&id=34&l=en. Accessed 24 Oct 2016

Exiang W, the 4th Civil Chamber of the Supreme People's Court (2006a) Trial guide on foreign-related commercial and maritime cases. People's court press, 2006(1):90–95

Exiang W, the 4th Civil Chamber of the Supreme People's Court (2006b) Trial guide on foreign-related commercial and maritime cases. People's court press, 2006(1):103–104

Exiang W, the 4th Civil Chamber of the Supreme People's Court (2006c) Trial guide on foreign-related commercial and maritime cases. People's court press, 2006(2):75–82

Exiang W, the 4th Civil Chamber of the Supreme People's Court (2008a) Trial guide on foreign-related commercial and maritime cases. People's court press, 2008(2):120–124

Exiang W, the 4th Civil Chamber of the Supreme People's Court (2006d) Trial guide on foreign-related commercial and maritime cases. People's court press, 2009(1):226–227

Exiang W, the 4th Civil Chamber of the Supreme People's Court (2009) Trial guide on foreign-related commercial and maritime cases. People's court press, 2009(2):75–86

Exiang W, the 4th Civil Chamber of the Supreme People's Court (2010a) Trial guide on foreign-related commercial and maritime cases. People's court press, 2010(1):71–75

Exiang W the 4th Civil Chamber of the Supreme People's Court (2010b) Trial guide on foreign-related commercial and maritime cases. People's court press, 2010(2):122–143

Exiang W the 4th Civil Chamber of the Supreme People's Court (2006e) Trial guide on foreign-related commercial and maritime cases. People's court press, 2011(1):164–174

[22]Bengbu Arbitration Commission, http://www.bbzcw.cn/page225?article_id=142. Accessed 17 June 2016.

Exiang W the 4th Civil Chamber of the Supreme People's Court (2001) Trial guide on foreign-related commercial and maritime cases. People's court press, 2011(1):175–180
Exiang W, the 4th Civil Chamber of the Supreme People's Court (2011) Trial guide on foreign-related commercial and maritime cases. People's court press, 2011(1):181–188
Exiang W, the 4th Civil Chamber of the Supreme People's Court (2008b) Trial guide on foreign-related commercial and maritime cases. People's court press, 2013(1):125–129

Part III
International Sale of Goods and Material Solutions

The Vienna United Nations Convention on Contracts for the International Sale of Goods: Applicability, Gaps and Implementation

Laura García Gutiérrez

1 Introduction

The 1980 Vienna Convention is a perfect example of success in the sphere of international trade regulations,[1] even more so if we take into account the number of times it has been ratified since being drafted in 1980. Eighty-three States,[2] with very different legal traditions and different economic and political regimes are currently parties to the Convention.[3] Moreover, some of these are key players in the international sale of goods, as is the case of the United States and China, which have been parties to the Convention since its inception, or the Russian Federation, for which the Convention entered into force on January 1, 1991. In fact, in the European Union, the only noncontracting States are the United Kingdom, Ireland, Portugal, and Malta, meaning there are only a few EU States that have not ratified the Convention. However, the fact that one such States is the United Kingdom is noteworthy, taking into account the important role it plays in international trade.

Among the States of the European Union that have applied the Convention the most, special mention should be made of Germany. On a global level, it has been used quite often in Russia and China, although, in both cases, for the most part through arbitration decisions.

However, this large number of ratifications would serve no purpose if the Convention was not being used in practice. At present and since its entry into force in January 1988, thousands of court and arbitration decisions have applied

[1] In this regard, see Ferrari (2008), p. 413.

[2] Data taken from http://www.uncitral.org.

[3] Not in vain, the Convention is equally authentic in six official languages: Arabic, Chinese, English, French, Russian, and Spanish.

L.G. Gutiérrez (✉)
University Autónoma of Madrid, Madrid, Spain
e-mail: laura.gutierrez@uam.es

N. Nord, G. Cerqueira (eds.), *International Sale of Goods*, China-EU Law Series 5,
DOI 10.1007/978-3-319-54036-8_7

it. Some authors have argued that it governs 80% of the contracts for the international sale of goods that are currently in force.[4]

Compared to the legal instruments discussed so far, the particularity of the Vienna Convention is that it is not a standard containing mainly conflict rules, i.e., provisions relating to contracts for the international sale of goods that establish a referral to a domestic legal system for the purpose of regulating these contracts. The 101 articles of the Vienna Convention mainly contain standard rules of law, i.e., substantive regulation (substantive law) for the matters covered. Its advantage, compared to domestic legal systems, is that it is specifically designed for international agreements rather than contracts that are solely of a domestic nature.

Significant negotiating efforts were therefore required from the different States that participated in its preparatory work, which started in the 1920s.[5] Its use has led to a clear reduction in the uncertainty arising from any international trade transaction due to a lack of advance knowledge regarding the applicable law, except when an express choice is made.

However, it must be borne in mind that the Vienna Convention does not regulate all aspects relating to contracts for the international sale of goods. The Convention is divided into four parts. Part I contains certain general provisions and then defines the sphere of application of the Convention, as well as applicability criteria. Part II regulates the formation of a contract. Part III contains the substantive rules on sales law and, in particular, the rights and obligations of the buyer and seller. Part IV contains a set of final provisions that could be described as rules of public international law, including, inter alia, articles regulating the various possibilities of making declarations (reservations) with respect to the articles of the convention. Since not all of the issues that may arise in a sales transaction are regulated in the Convention, one of the issues I will discuss is how to close the legal gaps that may arise.

On the other hand, it should be noted that the Vienna Convention is not only relevant in those cases in which it is applicable; it has also contributed to the transformation of numerous domestic laws on the sale of goods.[6]

This paper emphasizes the role of the Convention as a uniform law and subsequently focuses on its sphere of application and the criteria determining its applicability. The manner in which legal gaps should be handled according to the Convention itself is then explained. Finally, certain decisions in which these criteria have been implemented are analyzed.

---

[4]Schwender and Muñoz (2011), p. 159.

[5]Schlechtriem (2010), p. 1.

[6]In terms of its impact on the modernization of domestic laws on sales in member states of the European Union, v. Ferrari (2008), p. 347.

2 The Vienna Convention of 1980 Is Uniform Substantive Law

The Vienna Convention of 1980 has a clear purpose: unification of the legal regime for the international sales of goods, in order to contribute to international trade through the removal of legal barriers.

The international sales of goods are private international cases, i.e., legal relationships between individuals with ties to various States. As evidenced by doctrine and case law, it is not considered appropriate to deal with this type of cases as if they were purely domestic relationships under private law. Therefore, as is known, there are various legislative techniques to regulate them.[7] The most widespread is the use of conflict rules that refer to a particular legal system, from among the several with which the case in question has ties. Although this is the most widespread regulation technique, it gives rise to two legal problems. Firstly, it generates some uncertainty in cross-border legal transactions. Therefore, in principle, each State has its own rules of conflict, and therefore, there is uncertainty regarding what legislation a judge will end up applying in case of a dispute. Secondly, once a specific legal system is applied to a private international case, this case becomes somewhat "distorted." This is due to the fact that the rules of law to be applied are generally designed for cases that are purely domestic.

International uniform law, however, is substantive law designed specifically for private international cases, i.e., it contains applicable rules comparable to any domestic rules of substantive law.[8] Consequently, this regulatory technique has clear advantages if compared with the conflict technique since it can help to alleviate these two problems. In the first place, the uncertainty as to the applicable law is reduced,[9] and therefore there is increased legal security, which fosters international trade transactions. However, the criteria for the application of the uniform rules of law need to be sufficiently clear so as not to give rise to the same uncertainty they sought to overcome. Later, whether or not the Vienna Convention achieves this aim will be discussed.

In the second place, uniform law has the advantage that is designed specifically for private international cases. And that in my view is the reason why it is the most appropriate solution for their regulation, i.e., the Vienna Convention contains regulation especially designed for international contracts and is best suited for the specific problems related to these contracts.

However, reaching an agreement on a uniform set of rules is a complex task. States must agree on the legal solutions, and this is not always easy. Therefore, the progress made in the framework of the international sale of goods following several

---

[7] See, for example, Calvo Caravaca and Carrascosa González (2015), p. 349 and ff.

[8] In this sense, see Ferrari et al. (2012), p. 403, marg. 14.

[9] In this same sense, see Schlechtriem (2010), p. 29.

years of negotiations within the United Nations Commission on International Trade Law (UNCITRAL) can be regarded as a significant achievement.

In any case, there is no point in adopting uniform rules of law if they are not applied uniformly by the courts.[10] UNCITRAL itself has attempted to collect all case law on the Convention in order to contribute to making sure it is uniformly applied through the use of the CLOUT system.

Another notable aspect of the Convention is that it is a *self-executing treaty*.[11] Therefore, it does not depend on the enactment of any type of domestic legislation.

3 Material Scope of the Convention: The Concept of the Sale of Goods

When explaining in which cases the Vienna Convention is applied, it is most appropriate to begin by determining to which type of contracts it applies, taking into account that it will be up to the courts to analyze ex officio if the Convention is applicable, both from this standpoint as well as that of the internationality of the contract and other criteria relating to its applicability.

Therefore, in determining when the Vienna Convention is applicable, reference should be made to the contracts included under the Convention, i.e., its scope *ratione materiae*.

In this regard, it is striking that its core concept is not expressly defined within the Convention. In the 101 articles of this Convention, there is no definition of sale of goods. Authors have pointed out two possible reasons for this omission. Some claim that this concept is so well defined in the various domestic laws that no definition is necessary. Others, however, understand that reaching an agreement on the characterization of the contract might have been too costly and therefore negotiations would have become entrenched to some extent.

Regardless of the reason for this absence, what is certain is that, in practice, it is necessary to characterize the contract for the Convention to be applied. However, doing so should not entail referring to any domestic law in particular, which would lead to a divergent interpretation of this uniform text. Rather, in accordance with the provisions of Article 7.1 of the Convention, an independent interpretation should be made.[12] For this purpose, there is agreement that it is most appropriate to refer to Articles 30 and 53 of the Convention, which regulate the rights and obligations of the buyer and seller, respectively. Therefore, in principle, a sale will be any synallagmatic contract in which one party (the seller) is required to deliver goods

[10]In this same sense, see Ferrari (2008), p. 418 y 41 and in Ferrari (2005), p. 3; Schlechtriem (2010), p. 41.

[11]See Schwender and Muñoz (2011), p. 190, marg. 15.

[12]In this same sense, see Schlechtriem (2010), p. 11.

and all related documents, in order to transfer their ownership to another party. The other party (buyer) agrees to pay a price in exchange for and to receive the goods.[13]

This definition implies that other relevant international trade contracts, such as distribution or franchise contracts, are excluded from the scope of the Convention. However, in connection with the latter, contracts of sale entered into for the purpose of providing goods to a franchisee could, in my view, be considered to be included.

However, to refine the concept of sale under the Convention, this definition needs to be completed on the basis of two facts. On the one hand, there are contracts that are clearly contracts of sale, but Article 2 of the Convention excludes these contracts for various reasons. On the other hand, there are contracts that are not actual contracts of sale in a classical sense because they involve other additional benefits to *dare*, but these contracts are included in accordance with the provisions of Article 3. These two precepts will be analyzed in greater detail below.

In effect, Article 2 excludes some contracts of sale from the material scope of the Convention for a variety of reasons. These exclusions are exhaustive, meaning that they have to be interpreted in a strict manner and do not extend beyond what has been expressly provided for in the article. Accordingly, there is no admissibility of analogies.

Consequently, the Convention firstly excludes contracts of sale with consumers, defined in terms of the purpose of the contract (Art. 2.a), i.e., sale of goods bought for personal, family, or household use (= subjective criterion). The main reason for this exclusion, as has been pointed out in the doctrine, is to avoid the interference of the rules contained in the Convention with domestic consumer protection laws. However, it is also argued that there is a practical reason for this exclusion: the lack of relevance of these operations in international trade. The Convention is essentially professional law.

In any case, the Vienna Convention will apply to the sale of goods to personal, family, or household goods if the seller neither knew nor ought to have known that the goods were bought for any such use. In this regard, it is necessary for attention to be paid to the time before or at the conclusion of the contract. The burden of proof in this regard, is placed upon the party that desires to have the Convention applied. In other words, it is up to this party to demonstrate, in both the preliminary treatment and content of the contract, that the seller could not reasonably know what use was going to be given to the goods.

Secondly, the Convention does not apply to sales by auction or on execution or otherwise by authority of law (Art. 2.b and c). Auctions, which are understood to be sales to the highest bidder, normally fall under a specific regime provided in the State in which this contract is entered into since it is the territory to which contracts of this type are most linked. The peculiarity of contracts of this type is their specific formation process since until the time of the award, the buyer is not known. Online auctions, for example, would not be excluded, according to the majority doctrine, because their link to a particular territory is not as strong.

[13]See Calvo Caravaca (1993), pp. 13–14.

In regard to sales on execution or otherwise by authority of law (Art. 2.c), the reason for the exclusion is that there is little room for negotiation by the parties as to the terms of the contract.

Thirdly, sales of stocks, shares, investment securities, negotiable instruments, or money are excluded. In this case, the exclusion is based on the goods sold under the contract, to the extent that what is relevant in these cases seem to be the rights embodied in the same, which are intangible assets. In the case of money, the exclusion does not extend to coins and bills that are no longer legal tender or that are sold due to their historical value.

Fourthly, the sales of ships, vessels, hovercraft, or aircraft are not included within the material scope of the Convention. The legal treatment of these assets is very similar to that of real estate, and they often require registration, which is the reason behind their exclusion. The explicit reference to hovercraft, which may seem surprising, is due to the fact that its legal classification is arguable, and it was necessary to make its assimilation to other property subject to exclusion in this article very clear. The exclusion of aircraft does not extend to its parts when sold separately.

Finally, contracts for the sale of electricity are also excluded due to the special features of this sector of international trade. Again, this exclusion must be interpreted in the strictest sense and may not be extended to other forms of energy, such as contracts for the sale of oil or gas.[14]

This concludes the negative side of the concept of contract of sale for the purposes of the Convention (= excluded contracts of sale). On the positive side, there are also contracts included within the material scope of the Convention in accordance with the provisions of Article 3 that are not actually contracts of sale. These are not classical contracts of sale because together with a basic benefit in the form of a *dare* (transfer of ownership of property), there is another supplementary benefit that involves a *facere*,[15] i.e., a positive action on the part of the seller.

Firstly, contracts for the supply of goods to be manufactured or produced by the seller are chiefly considered to be sales (Art. 3.1), unless the party that orders the goods undertakes to supply a "substantial part" of the materials necessary for such manufacture or production. Secondly, the Vienna Convention also applies to the so-called mixed contracts, which involve not only the delivery of a good by the seller but also the supply of labor or the provision of a service (Art. 3.2). However, excluded are cases in which the "preponderant part" of the obligations assumed by the seller consists in the supply of labor or other services.

Both the terms "substantial part" and "preponderant part" used in Article 3 of the Convention are inexact, and therefore they require interpretation and specification. According to the majority doctrine, the best criterion for interpreting these two notions is economic value because it is an objective criterion also used in case law.

---

[14]In fact, the exclusion of contracts of this type was rejected during the development stages of the Convention.

[15]See Schlechtriem (2010), p. 173.

For example, the provision of service would be considered a preponderant part according to Article 3.2 if it were to account for over 50% of the contract. However, the economic criterion is arguable.

In both cases, the burden of proof would be placed on the party that relies on the derogation to defend the application of domestic law. Therefore, in the absence of such proof, the application of the Convention would be assumed in this type of contracts.

On the other hand, reference needs to be made to the concept of "goods" to be taken into account within the scope of the Convention. According to the doctrine, this term relates only to tangible personal property[16] and excludes all intangible assets, such as intellectual or industrial property rights (trademarks, patents, copyrights, or *know-how*). Whether certain assets can be considered as goods is arguable and can pose problems. In this regard, the doctrine has debated over whether or not contracts for the sale of software should be included within the material scope of the Convention in the case of IT contracts.[17] However, authors tend to be in favor of their inclusion.

Finally, it should be borne in mind that the wordings of the articles of the Convention evidence that they were drafted when electronic commerce was not as common as nowadays. It follows that these provisions should be adapted to this new reality.[18]

4 Internationality of the Sale: Fundamental for the Application of the Convention

Having identified the contracts to which the Convention applies, it is important to indicate the cases under which these contracts are subject to regulation by the Convention. The Convention regulates those contracts for the sale of international goods that also meet the requirements stated in either Article 1.1.a or 1.1.b.

Article 1.1 sets forth when a contract is considered to be international for the purposes of the Convention. Of most relevance is that the parties to the contract have places of business in different States. Other factors such as whether the delivery is made to a foreign State or whether the contract was entered into in a foreign Sate are irrelevant for these purposes.

However, both parties are required to disclose that the sale is international. Also, the fact that the parties have places of business in different States must be known by both parties, in accordance with the provisions of Article 1.2 of the Convention. Otherwise, the Convention would be inapplicable, in accordance with the principle

[16]See Campuzano Díaz (2000), p. 99.

[17]See Bernstein and Lookfsky (2003), p. 19; Schlechtriem (2010), pp. 11 and 460.

[18]In this same sense, see Kroll and Perales (2011), p. 18, marg. 61.

of predictability. However, the parties are not required to have been aware of the applicability of the Convention as such.

The burden of proof, in this case, is not regulated in the Convention, but it seems most logical for this burden to be placed on the party that claims that the Convention does not apply. Attention should be paid to any dealings between, or from information disclosed by, the parties at any time before or at the conclusion of the contract.

Hence, the concept of place of business is fundamental to the rules of the Convention. However, no explicit definition can be found within the Convention for this concept either. Based on the preparatory work, though, it can be concluded that the place of business should be understood to be the center of operations, through which the business of an enterprise is carried on commonly and regularly with human resources and goods. Consequently, places of business cannot be sporadic presences as in the case of participations in a fair, an exhibition, or an occasional meeting. Furthermore, a place of business is not deemed to exist merely due to the fact that it has an agent or a distributor. Additionally, registration is not required.

On the other hand, there is agreement in the doctrine that the place of business must be independent enough to enter into contracts.

Article 10 of the Convention clarifies some issues relating to the concept of place of business and, more specifically, what happens when one of the parties has more than one place of business or no place of business.

In the first case, the Convention takes into consideration the place of business that has the closest relationship to the contract and its performance. Therefore, it may very well be the case that a contract is concluded with a place of business other than the one with the closest relationship to its performance, in which case the latter would be preferred to the former.

Finally, according to Article 10, if one of the parties has no place of business, reference is to be made to his habitual residence, a concept that is not explicitly defined in the Convention.

5 The Conditions of Applicability of the Convention

From what has been explained thus far, in order for the Convention to be applicable to a contract, it must be covered under the Convention and must also be of an international character. However, this is not enough for the Convention to be applied. The court must also verify that either one or the other condition of applicability provided for in Article 1 of the Convention is met. Hence, this is a convention that does not apply universally.

The two conditions for its applicability take into account different factors. Article 1.1.a sets forth a criterion of direct or immediate application of the Convention. According to this precept, the Convention will be applicable as long as the States in which the parties have their places of business are both contracting States.

Given the large number of States parties to the Convention, this situation is quite common in practice.

Even so, there will be cases in which both parties or at least one of the two has its places of business in noncontracting States. In such cases, the possibility of applying the Convention should not simply be ruled out because the second criterion of applicability might still be met, i.e., the so-called application mediated or indirect criterion. In accordance with Article 1.1.b of the Convention, the Convention will be applicable when in accordance with the choice of law rules of the *forum*, the law of a contracting State is applicable to the contract. In this case, therefore, whether or not the Convention is applicable depends on the law applicable to the contract. In the States of the European Union, the applicable law is to be determined in accordance with Rome I Regulation.[19]

This second criterion of applicability is more complex than the first. A sample of this complexity can be, for example, whether or not there is some margin for the renvoi mechanism.[20] In fact, some States did not like this option, which is why on the initiative of the Czechoslovak delegation the Convention includes the option of making a reservation in relation thereto (Art. 95 of the Convention).[21] This implies that the contracting and noncontracting States to the Convention shall apply the Convention where the law applicable to the contract is the law of a contracting State, unless the parties have expressly excluded its application in accordance with Article 6. However, the courts of a reserving State shall only apply the Convention on the basis of the criterion of direct applicability provided in Article. 1.1.a or when the parties are expressly submitted to it in exercise of their freedom of choice. Few States have made this reservation, particularly the United States, China, the Czech Republic, Slovakia, St. Vincent and the Grenadines, Singapore, and Armenia.

Controversy would arise from a case, which is not very common, but cannot be ruled out, where Article 11.1.a cannot be applied, for example, because one of the parties has its place of business in a noncontracting State and the other in a reserving contracting State, but in accordance with Article 1.1.b, the applicable law would be that of the reserving State. In this case, an interpretation consistent with the wording of Article 1 would lead to the application of the Convention by the courts of a contracting State. However, most of the doctrine understands that in a case like this, for the sake of international harmony, the courts of nonreserving contracting States would not apply the Convention either.[22] Unequal decisions would be avoided in this way.[23]

In this respect, when ratifying the Convention on December 21, 1989, Germany made an interpretative declaration in relation thereto, under which its courts will not

---

[19]Regulation 593/2008 of 17th of June 2008, *DO* L177, of 4th July 2008.

[20]See Oliva Bázquez (2002), p. 98; Schwender and Muñoz (2011), p. 213, marg. 34.

[21]There are other possibilities of making reservations, as is the case of Art. 92 of the Convention, which permits a contracting State to choose not to apply part II or part III.

[22]See Schlechtriem (2010), p. 43, marg. 38.

[23]See in this regard, Ferrari et al. (2012), p. 406.

apply the Convention in cases where the criterion of applicability of Article. 1.1.a. is not met by both parties, and the applicable law is the law of a State that has made the reservation to Article 95. Therefore, in the case of the German courts, the Convention would undoubtedly be derogated in this case although Germany is not a reserving State.

6 Freedom of Choice and Gaps

Despite the criteria for the applicability of the Convention explained above, it should be made clear that it is a discretionary law. In fact, freedom of choice is one of the principles embodied therein. In this regard, Article 6 enables the parties to exclude the application of this Convention or derogate from any of its provisions. The possibility of agreeing to the application of the Convention beyond the cases in which the criteria for its application are met should also be acceptable, although there is no express provision indicating so in its articles.

Exclusion of its application can be express or implied. In this regard, in my view, its exclusion could be considered implicit in those cases in which the parties expressly agree to the application of the law of a noncontracting State. An agreement to apply the law of a contracting State should, in my opinion, be interpreted not as an exclusion of the Convention but rather as a confirmation of its applicability.

Additionally, the Convention does not regulate all the legal problems that a contract of sale may pose. For example, it does not regulate the requirements for the validity of the contract, the effects of the contract with regard to the ownership of the property, representation, receivable clearing, the assignment of receivables arising from the contract, the assumption of debts, novation, confirming deposits, the effect of the contract on third parties, or prescription.[24] Therefore, it is not exhaustive and solely regulates the formation of the contract, the rights and obligations of the parties, and the remedies in case of breach of contract. Accordingly, guidelines will need to be established to take into account possible gaps. This issue is regulated in Article 7.2 of the Convention in the case of the so-called internal gaps.

In accordance with the provisions of this article, the recourse to domestic law is always a last resort. In the first place, the matter is to be settled in conformity with the general principles on which the Convention is based. These principles include, inter alia, the principle of freedom of choice (Art. 6), the lack of requirements as to form (Arts. 11 and 29.1), the facilitation of the contract as opposed to its possible termination (Arts. 25, 26, 34, 37, 47–49, 63, and 64), the obligation of cooperation between the parties for the performance of the contract (Arts. 32 and 60), the duty of communication of important aspects of the contract (Arts. 19.2, 21.2, 26, 39.1, and

[24] See Ferrari (2009), p. 90 and ff.

65), the duty of the parties not to contradict past behaviors (Arts. 16.2.b, 29.2, 47.2, and 63.2), the lack of entitlement to claim damages for damage that could have been prevented or mitigated (Arts. 77, 85, 86.1, 86.2, and 88.2).[25] If it is not possible to close the gap through the abovementioned principles, it is necessary to resort to the applicable law in accordance with the rules of conflict of the *forum*. Therefore, despite the fact that the Vienna Convention is applicable, domestic law determined in accordance with the rules of conflict of the *forum* continues to have an important role.

From my point of view, in those cases in which the Convention applies, referring to domestic law remains a last resort in the event of a legal gap. This means that if a question is regulated in the Convention but the solution proposed is not the same or is clearly opposed to the solution provided under domestic law, the solution provided under the Convention must prevail.

7 Application of the Convention

As already pointed out above, the number of court and arbitration decisions that have applied the Convention is quite high, and there have already been thousands of them. Also mentioned previously was the importance of ensuring that the interpretation of the Convention is uniform so as not to defeat its main purpose: promoting international transactions through the unification of law on international cases.

Among the countries that have used the Convention is China, which signed the Convention on September 30, 1981, and approved it on December 11, 1986, it entering into force on January 1, 1988 (date of general entry into force of the Convention). In particular, it has been used by Chinese arbitration institutions such as the *China International Economic and Trade Arbitration Commission (CIETAC)*.

For example, there are quite a few cases of direct applicability of the Convention (Art. 1.1.a) by the CIETAC, such as the case of copper (decision of 8 July 2003) in which a buyer with a place of business in China and a seller in the United States signed a series of contracts for the purchase of copper.

In other cases, the Convention was applied as a result of the provisions of Article 1.1.b, i.e., although both parties did not have a place of business in contracting States, the applicable law was that of the contracting State. For example, in a decision handed down on June 30, 1999, there was a Chinese seller of peppermint oil and a buyer in the UK. The United Kingdom is not a party to the Convention. However, the Convention applied given that the law applicable to the contract was Chinese Law and China is a contracting State.

Among the decisions handed down by the CIETAC, there are cases of closing gaps by resorting to the rules of domestic law laid down in the legal system

[25]See Campuzano Díaz (2000), p. 82.

applicable to the contract. For example, mention should be made to a decision handed down on September 20, 2006, in which there was a Chinese buyer and a Belgian seller. The curious thing is that the law considered applicable by the arbitration court was Chinese rather than Belgian law, since China was considered to be the most closely linked to the contract.

References

Bernstein H, Lookfsky J (2003) Understanding the CISG in Europe. Kluwer Law Int, La Haya, Londre, Nueva York

Calvo Caravaca AL (1993) Consideraciones en torno al art. 1 de la Convención de Viena de 1980 sobre compraventa internacional de mercaderías. In: Hacia un nuevo orden internacional y europeo. Homenaje al Profesor M. Díez de Velasco, Tecnos, Madrid, pp 1329–1348

Calvo Caravaca AL, Carrascosa González J (2015) Derecho Internacional Privado, vol 1, 15th edn. Comares, Granada

Campuzano Díaz B (2000) La recepción del Convenio de viena de 11 de abril de 1980 en el ámbito de la compraventa internacional de mercaderías. Univ. de Sevilla, Sevilla

Ferrari F (ed) (2005) *Quo vadis* CISG? Bruylant/FEC/Sellier, Brussels/Paris/Munich

Ferrari F (2008) The CISG and its impact on National Legal Systems. Sellier, Munich

Ferrari F (2009) Fuentes aplicables a la compraventa internacional de mercaderías. Bosch, Barcelona

Ferrari F, Kieninger E-M, Mankowski P, Otte K, Saenger I, Schulze G, Staudinger A (2012) Internationales Vertragsrecht, 2nd edn. Beck, Munich

Kroll M, Perales V (eds) (2011) UN convention on contracts for the international sale of goods (CISG) commentary. Beck, Munich

Oliva Bázquez F (2002) Compraventa internacional de mercaderías (Ámbito de aplicación del Convenio de Viena de 1980). Tirant lo Blanch, Valencia

Schlechtriem S (2010) Commentary on the UN convention on the international sale of goods, 3rd edn. Oxford University Press, Oxford

Schwender I, Muñoz E (2011) Comentario sobre la Convención de las Naciones Unidas sobre contratos de compraventa internacional de mercaderías, vols I y II. Thomson Reuters, Pamplona

The Unidroit Principles of International Commercial Contracts in the Sino-European Sale of Goods Contracts

Gustavo Cerqueira

Merchandise exports from World Trade Organization members totaled US $16.5 trillion in 2015[1] and concerns dealers from over 200 nations and its diverse legal orders.[2] This diversity makes international trade highly complex.[3] It is within this context that lawyers need to choose the applicable law to sale contracts by comparing different national laws.

There are, however, some international uniform law instruments at their disposal: the 1980 United Nations convention on contracts for the international sale of goods (hereinafter "CISG") and the Unidroit principles of international commercial contracts (hereinafter "Unidroit Principles") are among the most important ones.

The Unidroit Principles set forth general rules that are basically conceived for international commercial contracts. But, unlike the CISG, they have no binding force in law. For this reason, they are often referred to as *soft law*.[4] They have been

[1]World Trade Organization, World Trade Statistical Review 2016, Merchandise trade and trade in commercial services.

[2]Top figures include North American and European, but also countries arising from transition economies from different points of the globe—particularly Brazil, China, India, Russia and some African countries. See, World Trade Organization, World Trade Statistical Review 2016, Statistical table.

[3]Brödermann (2011), p. 589.

[4]Bonell (2005a), p. 229: "'[s]oft law' is understood as referring in general to instruments of a normative nature with no legally binding force, and which are applied only through voluntary acceptance (. . .)."

G. Cerqueira (✉)
Faculty of Law, University of Reims Champagne-Ardenne, Reims, France
e-mail: gustavo.cerqueira@univ-reims.fr

N. Nord, G. Cerqueira (eds.), *International Sale of Goods*, China-EU Law Series 5,
DOI 10.1007/978-3-319-54036-8_8

prepared by a group of independent experts and set up by the International Institute for the Unification of Private Law—Unidroit.[5]

First published in 1994, the Unidroit Principles might soon celebrate their fourth edition. This new version will probably contain a Preamble and 213 articles[6] structured in 11 chapters. These last concern the general part of contract law and cover general provisions; formation; validity; interpretation; content, including third party rights and conditions; performance, including hardship and new dispositions on termination for compelling reason; nonperformance and remedies; set-off; assignment of rights; transfer of obligations and assignment of contracts; limitation periods; and plurality of obligors and of obligees. Each article is complemented by official comments and, where appropriate, by factual illustrations that explain the reasons for the black letter rule and the different ways it operates in practice. As Pr. Laura Gutierrez has exposed, with such a large scope, the Unidroit Principles cover a number of subjects not treated by the CISG.[7]

As a soft law instrument, the Unidroit Principles inaugurate an innovative approach to the law governing international contracts. Product of legal scholars from the major legal systems and geopolitical areas of the world, the Unidroit Principles is a result of intensive comparative legal research and debate.[8] They reflect the consensus of respectful scholars of both common law and civil law traditions and represent the general tendency of the development of contract law. For this reason, they are deemed,[9] alongside the CISG,[10] the foundation for an eventual future global code for international commercial contracts, proposed in 2012 by the Swiss delegation to the United Nations Commission on International Trade Law.[11] Furthermore, the Unidroit Principles have influenced legislators worldwide over the years,[12] as shown in the 1999 reform of the Chinese contract

[5]With its seat in Rome, the Unidroit is an intergovernmental organization established in 1926 as an auxiliary organ of the League of Nations. Composed of 63 member States, the Unidroit studies needs and methods for modernizing, harmonizing, and coordinating private and in particular commercial laws between States and groups of States. It formulates uniform law instruments, rules, and Principles to achieve those objectives (Article 1 of the Unidroit Statut).

[6]As opposed to the 120 articles of the 1994 edition, 185 articles of the 2004 and 211 of the 2010.

[7]See in this book, Gutierrez, The Vienna United Nations Convention on Contracts for the International Sale of Goods: applicability, gaps and implementation.

[8]Bonell (2005b), p. 26.

[9]Gabriel (2013), pp. 661–680.

[10]Ramberg (2013), pp. 681–690; Dennis (2014), pp. 114–151.

[11]UNCITRAL, Possible Future Work in the Area of International Contract Law: Proposal by Switzerland on Possible Future Work by UNCITRAL in the Area of International Contract Law, 45th session, New York, 25 June–6 July 2012, Doc A/CN.9/758 (8 May 2012). See Vill. L. Rev. (2013) 58(4), which is entirely dedicated to this issue. See also, Schwenzer (2016), pp. 60–74; Bonell (2001), pp. 87–100; Lando (2005), pp. 379–401.

[12]See, e.g., Estrella Faria (2016), pp. 238–270.

law,[13] the 2002 reform of the German contract law,[14] and recently the 2016 French reform of the law of obligations.[15]

More particularly, the Unidroit Principles emerge in a context where the diffusion of *model laws* and *Principles* contribute to renewing public international law (promotion of soft law instruments), comparative law (elaboration of a general model of regulation in a codified instrument), and private international law (new ways to organize the coexistence of rules of different nature—*hard law* and *soft law*; extension of private autonomy).[16]

Notwithstanding their prestige as a well-adapted a-national source for international commercial contracts, 22 years after their first edition the Unidroit Principles' application in international dispute resolution is rather modest.[17] Indeed, figures are not impressive, and only a very few decisions refer in one-way or another to the Unidroit Principles.[18] This is particularly the case in disputes related to Sino-European contracts of sale of goods.[19] It is also true that State court judges apply the Unidroit Principles as often as arbitrators, even though most arbitral awards referring to them remain unpublished.[20]

Recent developments in the Chinese conflict of laws rules on international contracts should, however, foster the use of the Unidroit Principles in contracts not subject to arbitration. Since it offers new perspectives for the Chinese and European companies concerning the applicable law to their sale of goods contracts, it seems legitimate to question which role could the Unidroit Principles play in this field.

It implies to opt for a prospective approach, *i. e.*, "to penetrate to some extent into disquieting realm of forecasts and hypotheses."[21] Sure, lawyers may not be the most reliable source to treat prospects due to their poor ability to predict the future. But "it is not forbidden, however, to venture therein prudently," as stated B. Goldman.[22]

[13]Zhang and Huang (2000), pp. 429–440; Li-Kotovtchikhine (2002), pp. 113–163; Shaohui (2003), pp. 219–230; (2008), pp. 153–178.

[14]Brödermann (2012), p. 311.

[15]Rapport au Président de la République relatif à l'ordonnance n° 2016-131 du 10 février 2016 portant réforme du droit des contrats, du régime général et de la preuve des obligations, *JORF* n° 0035 du 11 février 2016, Texte n° 25. See also: Réforme du droit des contrats: 3 questions à Carole Champalaune (Directrice des affaires civiles et du Sceau): http://www.textes.justice.gouv.fr/dossiers-thematiques-10083/loi-du-170215-sur-la-simplification-du-droit-12766/reforme-du-droit-des-contrats-3-questions-a-carole-champalaune-27931.html. Accessed 10 June 2016; Barbier (2016), p. 247.

[16]So Fauvarque-Cosson (2014), pp. 271–272.

[17]Consulting the annual ICC International Court of Arbitration Bulletin, it is not difficult to note that a choice of a national law corresponds to the most recurrent solution in international contracts containing a choice of law, at least for those subject to an ICC arbitration—about 97%. See, lastly: Cuniberti (2016), p. 773.

[18]See, Agrò (2011), pp. 719–733; Michaels (2014), p. 650.

[19]See, for instance, Manjiao (2010), pp. 5–36.

[20]Michaels (2014), p. 649 and ff.

[21]Goldman (1963), p. 382.

[22]Goldman (1963), p. 382.

Taking all these elements into account, the projection of the roles that the Unidroit Principles may play in the framework of Sino-European sale of goods (2) invites us to examine first the roles they have played in disputes within this framework until today (1).

1 State of the Art

The study of the actual state of applicability of the Unidroit Principles in the Sino-European trade of goods (Sect. 1.1) and of their concrete application in disputes between Chinese and European companies (Sect. 1.2) shows the level of development achieved by these principles and offers the keys for a prospective analyses.

1.1 Applicability of the Unidroit Principles to Sino-European Sale of Goods Contracts

In international trade, the certitude of the applicable law and the enforcement of specific rules is a necessity.[23] In this regard, as a binding law, once international conventions are ratified, they have the advantage of instant uniformity and enforceability.[24]

As far as the Unidroit Principles are concerned, they shall, according to their Preamble, be applied when the parties have agreed that they govern their contract. It should be especially the case—states the Preamble, although it is largely questionable[25]—when the parties have agreed that their contract is governed by general principles of law, the *lex mercatoria*, or similar. The parties may also agree that the Unidroit Principles should be used to interpret or supplement international uniform law instruments, such as the CISG, as well as to interpret or supplement domestic law. In these last hypotheses, the Unidroit Principles can be used in a dispute—be it litigated or arbitrated—regardless of previous agreements by the parties. Finally, in arbitration, they may also be applied when the parties have not chosen any law to govern their contract or in *ex aequo et bono* arbitrations.

Notwithstanding, an agreement to use a particular set of soft rules such as the Unidroit Principles is not self-enforcing but rather requires some domestic or supranational law for its enforcement before the judicial courts. In many

[23] Gabriel (2013), p. 676.

[24] Gabriel (2013), p. 676.

[25] Indeed, the assimilation of the Unidroit principle into the *lex mercatoria* is disputed. See Seraglini (2003), pp. 1101–1166, n° 11–22. Refusing such an assimilation: Award ICC n° 9474 (2001), 60–67, Award ICC n° 7375 (1996), A-1 A-69, Award ICC n° 9029 (1998), 88–96, mentioned by the author.

circumstances, this could lead to uncertainty when parties realize that the governing terms of the agreement might not be enforced according to their expressed wishes.

Today, the use of the Unidroit Principles in the Sino-European trade relations is possible to some extent. While in Europe their application remains basically limited to arbitral disputes, the evolution of Chinese conflict of laws in civil and commercial matters will allow parties to overcome the traditional restrictions for choosing such Principles to govern their contracts—either primarily or subsidiarily.

Traditional restrictions in Chinese Law still running in European Law (Sect. 1.1.1) and new solutions within Chinese conflict of laws system (Sect. 1.1.2) are matters we will consider respectively.

1.1.1 Traditional Restrictions Resulting from Conflict of Laws Rules

Traditionally, for both Chinese and European conflict of law systems, a *soft law* instrument is not considered as law. That is the main reason justifying the parties' interdiction for choosing the Unidroit Principles. Despite such a formal interdiction, a positive tendency for the acceptance and use of Unidroit Principles preceded the new solutions at the Chinese conflict of law level. Let us look first at the main reason for interdiction (Sect. 1.1.1.1) before looking into the positive features on acceptance of the implementation of the Unidroit Principles (Sect. 1.1.1.2).

1.1.1.1 Main Restriction: Soft Law Is No Law

Regardless of the nationality of the court hearing a dispute—be it Chinese or European—when concerning a contract of sale of goods between a Chinese company and a European company, the conflict of law rules, traditionally, do not accept stipulations designating a non-State law.

In the European Union, two instruments regulate the law applicable to contractual obligations: the 1980 Rome Convention and the 2008 Rome I Regulation. The first is applicable to contracts concluded between April 1, 1991, and December 16, 2009, while the second is applicable to contracts concluded from December 17, 2009.[26] Since Article 3 of Rome I Regulation and the Rome Convention use the word "law" as the subject of a choice, the choice of a non-State rule is not admitted. Consequently, faced with a demand designating the Unidroit Principles, the judge will consider that the parties made no choice. He will then use the conflict of law rules applicable in the absence of a choice. This means that contracts for the sale of goods concluded under Rome I Regulation, for example, shall be governed by the law of the country where the seller has his habitual residence, according to Article 4, §1, *a*. If a commercial dispute is brought before a French court, as well as a

[26]International contracts concluded before 1 April 1991 are subject to the national or conventional conflict of law rules that were in force in each European Member State.

Danish, an Italian, a Finnish, or a Swedish court, the solutions are similar when applying the Hague Convention of June 15, 1955, on the law applicable to international sales of goods (Articles 2 and 3).[27]

From a European point of view, these restrictions do not concern contracts subject to arbitration since arbitrators, in most cases, are not bound to conflict of law systems.[28] Moreover, many regulations of arbitration do not refer to "national law" but refer to "rules of law" as the applicable law. "Rules of law" is often understood as nothing more than a placeholder term for a broader concept of law that includes non-State law.[29] Such provisions can be found, for example, in the rules of arbitration used by the French International Chamber of Commerce (hereinafter ICC)[30] and by the London Court of International Arbitration[31] or even by national laws on arbitration, such as the French Code of Civil Procedure.[32] By giving effect to the contractual parties' will, the arbitration tribunal takes no risk of refusal of recognition and execution of its award because, at least under the New York Convention of June 10, 1958, on Recognition and Enforcement of Foreign Arbitral Awards,[33] the decision on the applicable substantive law cannot be a reason for the refusal of an enforcement of an award.[34]

In China, before the 2010 new Private International Law Statute,[35] the parties could not choose non-State sources. The word "Law" was systematically understood as equivalent to State law in the various conflict of law rules of legislative texts. An example is the Contract Law of March 1999, which contains particular

[27] See in this book Nord, Identification of the applicable law in China and in Europe.

[28] Derains (2002), pp. 9 at 12.

[29] Michaels (2014), p. 647 and ff.

[30] Article 21 of the 2012 ICC Rules of Arbitration determines in paragraph 1: "The parties shall be free to agree upon the rules of law to be applied by the arbitral tribunal to the merits of the dispute. In the absence of any such agreement, the arbitral tribunal shall apply the rules of law which it determines to be appropriate".

[31] Article 14.5. of the 2014 LCIA Rules determines: "The Arbitral Tribunal shall have the widest discretion to discharge these general duties, subject to such mandatory law(s) or *rules of law* as the Arbitral Tribunal may decide to be applicable; and at all times the parties shall do everything necessary in good faith for the fair, efficient and expeditious conduct of the arbitration, including the Arbitral Tribunal's discharge of its general duties."

[32] Article 1511: "The arbitral tribunal shall decide the dispute in accordance with the rules of law chosen by the parties or, where no such choice has been made, in accordance with the rules of law it considers appropriate. In either case, the arbitral tribunal shall take trade usages into account".

[33] 330 United Nations Treaty Series, 38.

[34] The reference in Art. V(1) lit. (a) of the New York Convention to the validity of the agreement under the law chosen by the parties or, failing such indication, under the law of the country where the award was made, refers solely to the arbitration agreement as defined in Article II(1) of the New York Convention.

[35] See, *e. g.*, Nord and Cerqueira (2016), pp. 79–104; Nord and Cerqueira (2011), pp. 70–101; Cerqueira (2011), pp. 181–228; Cerqueira et al. (2011), pp. 52–56; Chen and Bertrand (2011), pp. 375–389; Tu (2011), pp. 563–590; Huo (2011), pp. 1063–1093; Pissler (2012), pp. 1–46; Cavalieri Renzo and Franzina (2012).

choice of law provisions for foreign-related contracts. According to its Article 126: "[p]arties to a foreign-related contract may choose the applicable law to deal with the dispute arising from their contract except where otherwise provided." If this provision is silent as to whether the Principles could be considered as "applicable law," the interpretation of the Supreme People's Court on applicable law issues of June 2007 provides that "[t]he law applicable to foreign-related contracts related to civil and commercial matters refers to the substantive law in related countries or regions, excluding the conflict of law and procedural law." It was then clear that under Chinese law, the law governing a contract should be a "State law or regional law" rather than "rules of law"; therefore, the Unidroit Principles could not be qualified as applicable law.

In Chinese arbitration practices, the situation was not much different. A 2010 study on the application of the Unidroit Principles in China has shown that the Chinese arbitration regime was not sufficiently receptive of the Principles.[36] The main problem concerned the grounds upon which the Principles can be applied. Unlike the various leading arbitration rules, national laws and international instruments already mentioned, the arbitrators in China must follow the prescribed conflict of law rules to identify the applicable substantive law. This method is adopted by the CIETAC rules and by many, if not all other Chinese arbitration commissions. In particular, Article 49, paragraph 1 of CIETAC rules, which reproduces its former Article 41-1, provides that "1. [t]he arbitral tribunal shall independently and impartially render a fair and reasonable arbitral award based on the facts of the case and the terms of the contract, in accordance with the law, and with reference to international practices." The reference to "in accordance with the law" requires the arbitrators to base their decisions on special Chinese provisions involving foreign elements. As far as an international sale of goods is concerned, the arbitrator shall first follow the *lex loci arbitri*, *i. e*., 1994 Chinese Arbitration Law and 1991 Chinese Civil Procedural Law as amended in 2007. None provides an operable conflict of law rules. For example, Article 7 of the Chinese Arbitration Law, applicable to foreign-related arbitration according to its Article 65, only provides that "[i]n arbitration, disputes shall be resolved on the basis of facts, in compliance with the law and in an equitable and reasonable manner." Considering the silence of Chinese arbitrations rules, the arbitrator must identify the applicable law by following the conflict of law rules. Furthermore, the reference to "international practices," which are applicable, according to Article 142, paragraph 3 of 1986 Chinese General Principles of the Civil Law, only for interpretational or supplementary purposes, does not imply the application of the Unidroit Principles.[37] It is clearly understood that the Unidroit Principles are definitely not a

[36]Manjiao (2010), pp. 5–36.

[37]Xiao and Long (2009), p. 202; *contra* Li-Kotovtchikhine (2002), p. 123.

restatement of such practice,[38] even if an arbitral court in China[39] and others elsewhere have already referred to them as such.[40]

Anyway, as far as an international sale of goods is concerned, two cases involving Chinese and European parties reported by UNILEX show the impact of legal restrictions to the choice of a non-State law on the CIETAC practice. The first case, between a Chinese claimant and a Swiss defendant,[41] dates from 2004. Since the parties made no choice of law—which would anyhow be restricted to a State law or a regional law, with limited room for "international practices"—the tribunal decided to apply the CISG in conjunction with Chinese law. In order to justify its decision to apply the CISG, the tribunal argued first that both countries were contracting States of this convention. As CISG does not provide a complete regulation on the disputed issues, the tribunal decided to fulfill the gap applying the Chinese law. There are two reasons for the tribunal's decision: first, the Chinese law was implicitly chosen by the parties since they agreed to China as the place for arbitration; second, "in view of the considerable differences among domestic laws in this field, the gap could not be filled by virtue of Article 7.4.13 of the Unidroit Principles—agreed payment for non-performance—but only by recourse to the otherwise applicable domestic law." The second case dates from September 2005. It was a dispute between a French and a Chinese party, who made no choice of law.[42] The tribunal applied the CISG since it was in force in both States. The tribunal rejected the French party's request to apply the Unidroit Principles on the amount of interest due to delayed payment, holding that since the Principles were neither an international convention nor a subject of a parties' choice, it lacked both legal and contractual grounds for their application.[43]

Despite the Unidroit Principles' unfavorable status in China and Europe in a recent period, a positive tendency can be noticed to their acceptance as applicable law in both regions.

---

[38]Michaels (2014), p. 647 and ff.

[39]China International Economic and Trade Arbitration Commission, unknown date (2007).http://www.unilex.info/case.cfm?id=1208. Accessed in 14 juin 2016. See also Huang (2008), pp. 135–136; Lefebvre and Jiao (2002), p. 148. For a criticism of such an approach: Michaels (2014), p. 649.

[40]See some decisions mentioned by Michaels (2014), p. 649.

[41]China International Economic and Trade Arbitration Commission, September 2004, n° 0291-1: http://www.unilex.info/case.cfm?id=1441. Accessed in 14 juin 2016.

[42]China International Economic and Trade Arbitration Commission, 2 September 2005. http://www.unilex.info/case.cfm?id=1355. Accessed in 14 juin 2016.

[43]Pursuant to Pr. Chi Manjiao, what seems quite conflicting is that the tribunal let us suppose that the Unidroit Principles could have been applied on the ground of the parties' will. To justify such paradox, the tribunal tried to draw a clear distinction between the wording "apply the Principles" and "refer to the Principles", which was expressly mentioned in the sentence, to avoid leaving an impression that the Principles were effectively applied as applicable law Manjiao (2010), p. 29.

1.1.1.2 Some Windows for Acceptance of the Unidroit Principles

At the outset, the judicial practice in China reveals some applications or the taking into account of the Unidroit Principles despite their weak status in that legal order. In a dispute concerning a termination of a domestic lease contract on account of hardship, the *Shaoguan Intermediate People's Court* has referred to the Unidroit Principles to endorse the conformity of Chinese law solutions in this matter with international standards.[44] In other 12 cases, the Unidroit Principles were only referred to by Chinese courts in "case comments."[45] The particularity of those cases is that the disputes were based on a purely domestic contract instead of a foreign-related contract. As pointed out by Pr. Chi Manjiao, the reference to the Principles in the "case comments" could imply that the Principles may serve as "background law" in China.[46] By doing so, the courts intend to confirm that their decision, made under Chinese contract law, is in line with the "international standards" as the ones represented by the Principles.[47]

At the European level, Article 3 of Rome I Regulation and the Rome Convention and Article 2 of the 1955 Hague Convention have not considered the possibility of choosing a non-State rule. Nonetheless, some inflexions can be found in the recitals of Rome I Regulation.[48] Summarizing, recital n° 13 states that "[t]his Regulation does not preclude parties from incorporating by reference into their contract a non-State body of law or an international convention," while recital n° 14 provides that "[s]hould the [European Union] adopt, in an appropriate legal instrument, rules of substantive contract law, including standard terms and conditions, such instrument may provide that the parties may choose to apply those rules."

Furthermore, according to Pr. Fauvarque-Cosson, the 2015 Hague Principles on choice of law in international commercial contracts may, to some extent, reinforce the normativity of the Unidroit Principles.[49] Article 3 of the Hague Principles allows the choice of *rules of law* that are generally accepted in an international, supranational, or regional level as a neutral and balanced set of rules, unless the law of the forum provides otherwise. The Unidroit Principles fill with perfection such requirements. For the author, despite the limitations of Rome I Regulation, Article 3 of the Hague Principles seems to find full application on the ground of the liberal case law of the *Cour de cassation*. Indeed, since the judge is not obliged to apply the

---

[44]Shaoguan Intermediate People's Court, 28.04.2005, *Hengxing Company v. Guangdong Petrochemical Subsidiary Company*. An abstract of this case is available at http://www.unilex.info/case.cfm?id=1120. Accessed in 11 June 2016.

[45]In China, "case comments" are internal court circulars and have no binding force in law. Hence, the Principles served a scholarly or educational purpose—often published and intended as guidelines for judges (particularly those of the lower courts)—and are not effectively applied to resolve the disputes. See Manjiao (2010), p. 23.

[46]See *infra* 3.2.

[47]Manjiao (2010), p. 23.

[48]See in this book Nord, Identification of the applicable law in China and in Europe.

[49]Fauvarque-Cosson (2014), p. 280 and ff.

conflict of law rules on contract law unless requested by the parties and since the parties are free to choose a substantive law and invoke it before the judge, it would be natural that the parties' choice reaches further than the national substantive laws, reaching also the conflict of laws and the a-national laws, as does Article 3 of the Hague Principles. Such an approach—which is still to be confirmed by the French tribunals—implies the abandonment of the rule settled in 1950 by the *Cour de cassation*, by which "all contract is necessarily attached to a State Law."[50]

Anyway, besides the European arbitration practice, the judicial practice in European countries shows that the Unidroit Principles are often invoked by litigators or by judges even when they have not been chosen. By far, the biggest portion of decisions are those in which the Unidroit Principles are used for interpretation and supplementation of international law and, even more frequently, domestic law.[51] For example, the Unidroit Principles may be used to interpret and supplement the CISG on issues unanswered by the national law, subsidiarily applicable according to Article 7 CISG. Thus, a very recent decision held by the French *Cour de cassation* shows how the acceptance of the hardship's doctrine—which until the 2016 reform of the law of obligations[52] was expressly refused by this Court[53]—could be implicitly envisaged in a particular case, thanks to Unidroit Principles, when invoked by one of the claimants.[54] This is not without importance considering that the contracts concluded before October 1, 2016, remain governed by the prior contractual law rules of the French *Code civil*.

This positive tendency for a greater use of the Unidroit Principles as the chosen applicable law by the parties is reinforced today by the advent of a new favorable room in China.

1.1.2 Recent Developments in Chinese Conflict of Law Rules: New Perspectives on the Applicability of the Unidroit Principles

Evolutions in Chinese conflict of law rules create a new favorable room in which the Unidroit Principles have become available as the applicable law in the sense of private international law. Indeed, Article 3 of the 2010 Private International Law Statute—which provides that "[i]n accordance with statutory provisions, the parties may expressly choose the law applicable to a civil relationship involving foreign elements"—must be interpreted as permitting the designation of international

[50]Cass. Ch. Civ., sect. civ., 21 juin 1950, *Messageries maritimes*.

[51]Michaels (2014), p. 647 and ff.

[52]See: new article 1195 of the Civil Code.

[53]Cass. Civ., 6 March1876, *Canal de Capronne*.

[54]Cass. Com., 17 February 2015, n° 12-29550, 13-18956, 13-20230. It shall be noted that the same Commercial Chamber has already showed some inflexions to the *Canal de Capronne* jurisprudence in order to sanction on the basis of good faith, the contractor, which benefits of the changing of circumstances, for refusing to renegotiate the contract.

customs or international conventions.[55] The solution is reinforced by Article 9 of the Court's interpretation of December 10, 2012, according to which "[w]here the parties in their contract refer to an international convention which is not effective in the PRC, the People's Court may determine their rights and duties pursuant to it, unless its provisions violate the socio-public interests or the mandatory rules contained in laws and administrative regulations of the PRC."

Therefore, because the parties may choose the law applicable to their contract,[56] they may refer to an international convention to govern it, which is not yet in force in China or other countries. This is clearly a non-State rule because it has not been elaborated by a national legislator and has not or not yet been included in the Chinese system. That confirms, *a fortiori*, that the parties can henceforth choose the Unidroit Principles.[57]

This evolution may contribute to a reality change at least with regard to adjudication: the Unidroit Principles are rarely applied as the applicable law in the sense of private international law,[58] although this has been a major project since the beginning, supported by countless scholarly articles and a number of legislative proposals, as for example the draft for Rome I Regulation, which had provided for the choice of non-State law.[59]

From a Sino-European trade perspective, the importance of the evolution of the Chinese conflict of law system towards the acceptance of a choice of rule of law in international contracts shall, however, be relativized since the European private international law remains reluctant to such a liberal solution. Consequently, only arbitrated disputes and litigation before Chinese tribunals will benefit for sure from the new Chinese provisions.

Anyway, considering that the applicability of the Unidroit Principles in China and, to a certain extent, in some European countries has been reinforced, it is time to verify their concrete application until today in the Sino-European trade.

1.2 Application of the Unidroit Principles to Sino-European Sale of Goods Contracts

The application of the Unidroit Principles in disputes concerning a Chinese and a European party is rare. Since their first edition in 1994, very few pertinent cases are known. Indeed, only seven decisions in which the Unidroit Principles were applied

[55]See, *e. g.*, Pissler (2012), p. 10, and references quoted by this author at footnote 47; Huo (2011), p. 1085. Already before the advent of the 2010 Private International Law Statute: Shaohui (2004), p. 421 and references quoted by this author at footnote 6.

[56]Article 41 of the 2010 Private International Law Statute.

[57]Nord and Cerqueira (2016), pp. 90–91.

[58]Michaels (2014), p. 657.

[59]Michaels (2014), p. 663.

or considered by the tribunals have been reported by UNILEX. Since UNILEX is considered the main database for international case law, these figures can be taken as quite representative of the reality, even though most of arbitral awards, and the ones that might have eventually referred to such Principles, are unknown to the public.

Anyway, six from seven decisions were held on international sale of goods disputes. All of them were arbitral awards. From these six awards, two refused to apply and to even consider the Unidroit Principles. Finally, the other four awards have applied the Unidroit Principles on different grounds.

The two awards refusing to apply the Unidroit Principles have been mentioned previously in this text to illustrate the impact of legal restrictions to the choice of a non-State law on the CIETAC practice.[60] If the reluctance of Chinese arbitral practice shall evolve and, who knows, fade after the 2010 new Private international law Statute and the 2012 SPC's Opinion, arbitral awards confirming it are still unknown.

The four awards applying the Unidroit Principles to a Sino-European contract of sale of goods were held by arbitral tribunals, functioning under the auspices of arbitration centers in Europe. Two European countries are particularly concerned: Russia, which does not belong to the European Union, and the French ICC. True, this figure is not expressive. But it shows which role the Unidroit Principles played lately on international sale of goods disputes involving a Chinese and a European party.

In three of these four awards, the Unidroit Principles were used twice to supplement previous chosen national laws and once to supplement the CISG. In a fourth award, where the parties made no choice of law, the Unidroit Principles were applied, together with the national law of the arbitration's place. The details of these decisions can be analyzed by considering two ways in which the Principles intervene in the litigation.

As a supplement of the applicable law, the Unidroit Principles were applied on different grounds. Firstly, they were used as an *expression of "international practices"* in a case decided by ICC in 2000.[61] In this case, a Chinese company, entered into agreement with an East European car manufacturer for the provision and organization of after-sales service for vehicles delivered by the latter. Subsequently, the parties accused each other of having failed to comply with their obligations under the contract. The Chinese party initiated arbitration proceedings against the European manufacturer for breach of contract and requested both compensatory and punitive damages. Both parties agreed that Chinese law was the law governing the merits of the dispute but at the same time requested the arbitral tribunal to also apply the Unidroit Principles as an expression of international practices. The tribunal declared that it would base its decision on Chinese law

[60] See, *supra*, point Sect. 1.1.1.1.

[61] ICC International Court of Arbitration, sentence n° 10114, March 2000, Unkown parties. http://www.unilex.info/case.cfm?id=696. Accessed in 11 June 2016.

and on "international practices, including Unidroit Principles." As to the merits of the case, the tribunal rejected claimant's request for punitive damages, and in doing so, it pointed out that the concept of punitive damages was not known in Chinese contract law, nor it had found any international trade principle authorizing the award of punitive damages.

Secondly, they were used as an *expression of the Lex Mercatoria* in a case decided by the International Arbitration Court of the Chamber of Commerce and Industry of the Russian Federation in 2009.[62] In this case, a Russian company entered into a sales contract with a Chinese company. A dispute arose when the former requested from the latter to return the advance payment and to repay the costs of participating in settlement negotiations. The law of the Russian Federation governed the contract. However the arbitral tribunal, having found no specific regulation in that law addressing the issue at stake, referred to the Unidroit Principles as *lex mercatoria* in order to justify their subsidiary application to Russian Civil Law and in particular applied Article 7.4.8 on the duty to mitigate the harm caused by the nonperformance and the right to reimbursement of the expenses reasonably incurred.

Thirdly, the Unidroit Principles were used *as supplement to CISG* in a case decided by the International Arbitration Court of the Chamber of Commerce and Industry of the Russian Federation in 2013.[63] In this case, the sale of goods contract between a Russian company and a Chinese company was governed by the CISG. Nonetheless, the tribunal also applied the Russian Civil Law and the Unidroit Principles as a means of supplementing that convention. Reference was made to Articles 1.7 (Good faith and fair dealing)[64] and 5.1.3 (Cooperation between the parties)[65] of the Unidroit Principles.

As a main applicable law. In the absence of choice or request by the parties, the Unidroit Principles were applied only once, in an arbitral award held by the International Arbitration Court of the Chamber of Commerce and Industry of the Russian Federation in 2013.[66] In this case, the tribunal applied the Unidroit Principles as the law applicable to the substance of the dispute, without being

[62] International Arbitration Court of the Chamber of Commerce and Industry of the Russian Federation, 2 June 2009, n° 148. http://www.unilex.info/case.cfm?id=1552. Accessed in 11 June 2016.

[63] International Arbitration Court of the Chamber of Commerce and Industry of the Russian Federation, 16.07.2013, n° 177/2012. http://www.unilex.info/case.cfm?id=1807. Accessed in 11 June 2016.

[64] Article 1.7 (Good faith and fair dealing): "(1) Each party must act in accordance with good faith and fair dealing in international trade. (2) The parties may not exclude or limit this duty".

[65] Article 5.1.3 (Co-operation between the parties): "Each party shall co-operate with the other party when such co-operation may reasonably be expected for the performance of that party's obligations".

[66] International Arbitration Court of the Chamber of Commerce and Industry of the Russian Federation, 27 May 2013, n° 166/2012. http://www.unilex.info/case.cfm?id=1791. Accessed in 11 June 2016.

requested to do so by the parties (a Russian and a Chinese company). It referred in particular to Article 6.1.8 (2) of the Unidroit Principles, which states that in case of payment by transfer, the obligation of the obligor is discharged when the transfer to the obligee's financial institution becomes effective. The tribunal also applied the Russian Civil Code.

What do these decisions basically show? First, while the Chinese arbitral tribunal had refused to apply or even take the Unidroit Principles into account, the European arbitrations did it. Second, the International Arbitration Court of the Chamber of Commerce and Industry of the Russian Federation held three of the four decisions applying the Unidroit Principles. Yet Russia, like Turkey, is not considered fully as a European country despite its membership in the Council of Europe. Still, the reported arbitral Russian decisions concerned only Russian companies in their dispute with Chinese ones. From the four, only one reported decision concerns a "truly" Sino-European dispute on international sale of goods in which the Unidroit Principles were applied. Third, the role played by the Unidroit Principles to solve disputes between parties to a Sino-European sale of goods contract is effectively rare.

This reality makes us wonder about the Unidroit Principles' perspectives for the future.

2 Perspectives for the Future

The prospective approach ventured in this work implies considering two data. On one hand, the evolution of Chinese requirements for the application of the Unidroit Principles creates new room for the already existing competition between regional and global soft law instruments on contract law (Sect. 2.1). On the other hand, the role that Unidroit Principles played until now in the Sino-European contract of sale of goods confirms some surprising findings at global level exposed by scholars,[67] which settle that Unidroit Principles are basically a background law. The understanding of this reality leads us to question what should be their role in the future (Sect. 2.2).

2.1 Competition Between Soft Law Instruments on Contract Law

From a narrow point of view of their applicability, the competition between Unidroit and other international soft law instruments in the matters of contract is

[67] Michaels (2014), pp. 643–668.

very likely to occur (Sect. 2.1.1). In this case, the Unidroit Principles present some real advantages that should prevail (Sect. 2.1.2).

2.1.1 Potential Competition Between Soft Law Instruments

Under the argument that different domestic laws constitute obstacles to international trade, endeavors on the global and regional levels to the harmonization or unification of contract law are a reality. At global level, in 2012 the Swiss delegation made a proposal to the United Nations Commission on International Trade Law (hereinafter UNCITRAL) for the drafting of a global commercial code. At regional level, there are private academic initiatives from Asia and Latin America. In Europe, three important restatements result from the work of a group of experts: the Principles of European Contract Law,[68] the Common Contractual Principles[69]/ Common contractual terminology[70] and the Draft Common Frame of Reference—the DCFR.[71] Moreover, building on the DCFR, the European Commission published in October 2011 a proposal for a Regulation of the European Parliament and of the Council on a Common European Sales Law. Despite its legal nature, this regulation should be an opting-in instrument.[72]

In the global arena, the Unidroit Principles have not become the main model for international legislation as expected—except for the OHADA's draft contract code. Both the UNCITRAL proposal for a global commercial code and the proposed Principles of Asian Contract Law[73] have grown largely independent of them.[74] Also, even if other regional soft law instruments, such as the Principles of European Contract Law, the Draft Common Frame of Reference, and the proposal for Latin American Contract Law are closely linked to the Unidroit Principles, in their spirit and in their content they have some important differences. Furthermore, the European proposal for a regulation on Common European Sales Law, despite having been abandoned, presented a broader material scope also covering contracts with consumers.

Such nonbinding codifications differ in detail and also fulfill the requirements to be recognized as a valid parties' choice, at least from the Chinese conflict of law

---

[68]Also known as Lando Principle's: Lando and Beale (1999); Lando et al. (2003).

[69]Fauvarque-Cosson, Mazeaud (coord.), Wicker, Racine (dir.) (2008b).

[70]Fauvarque-Cosson, Mazeaud (coord.), Tenebaum (dir.) (2008a).

[71]Von Bar et al. (2008).

[72]In Europe, a few more private initiatives undertook similar projects, among them the Academy of European Private Lawyers (Pavia Group), which issued the preliminary draft for a European Code (2001) (see Gandolfi (2001) The Academy of European Private Lawyers and the Pavia Draft of a "European Contract Code"'. http://ec.europa.eu/consumers/cons_int/safe_shop/fair_bus_pract/cont_law/stake) and the Trento Common Core Project (see <www.common-core.org/). Accessed 18 June 2016.

[73]See Han (2013), pp. 589–599.

[74]Michaels (2014), p. 656 and ff.

perspective. The chances for them to be chosen make them potential competitors in the international arena, a phenomenon described some time ago.[75] Such a competition may even extend to treaties, such as the CISG, outside of their scope of application. Regarding the perspective of the Sino-European trade, the place that can be occupied by the Unidroit Principles seems to be a real question.

From a global point of view, we may agree with Pr. Ralf Michaels, who believes that none of the nonbinding existing transnational texts can claim ultimate authority.[76] Indeed, when both courts and legislators refer to the Unidroit Principles side by side with other non-State texts and even domestic legal texts, they look into these texts in an attempt to evaluate which view is more widespread and more convincing, instead of applying one at the expense of the other.[77] Notwithstanding such a hierarchical equivalence between the nonbinding existing or upcoming transnational texts, real advantages exist for the Unidroit Principles.

2.1.2 Real Advantages for the Unidroit Principles

First of all, Unidroit Principles have proved their utility not only as a model for domestic law making but also in the litigation and arbitration practices. Unlike these, there is no information of reported cases for the Principles of European Contract Law, even though the parties may choose them, at least in arbitration.[78]

Therefore, it is common sense that regional attempts to harmonize and unify general contract law could not fulfill the needs of international trade since different legal regimes in different regions lead rather to fragmentation, strongly marked by the laws of the respective countries involved.[79] For example, the DCFR was severely criticized for the general idea of the project, especially for the drafting and style, as well as for the specific solutions in the area of general contract and sales law.[80] In this regard, the Unidroit Principles have the advantage of having been drafted with a universal and not a regional perspective.[81] Some ICC awards make it clear when it comes to showing the adaptability of the Unidroit Principles to

[75]See Seraglini (2003), n° 2 and 19.

[76]Michaels (2014), p. 667.

[77]Ibid. Such a broad comparative survey lead by adjudicators is not rare, as illustrates a recent decision held by the Spanish Supreme Court, which cited, in matter of contract interpretation, not just Article 4.1 of the Unidroit Principles but also Article 236 of the Portuguese Civil Code, Article 1156 of the French Code Civil, Article 1362 of the Italian Civil Code, and Article 5:101 of the Principles of European Contract Law (Tribunal Supremo, Case n° 74/2012 (29 February 2012). http://www.unilex.info/case.cfm?id=1652. Accessed 11 June 2016). For other examples, see also Michaels (2014), pp. 651–652.

[78]Schwenzer (2016), p. 68.

[79]Schwenzer (2016), p. 68.

[80]Schwenzer (2016), p. 68.

[81]Gabriel (2013), p. 678.

international trade, especially for international sale of goods.[82] Indeed, from a Sino-European commercial relations perspective, it is particularly the case.

One of the rare decisions applying mainly the Unidroit Principles in a dispute between Chinese and European parties justifies such an application in the absence of a party choice using the following arguments: the Unidroit Principles have wide recognition and set out principles that in the tribunal's opinion offer a protection for contracting parties that adequately reflect the basic principles of commercial relations in most, if not all, developed countries; such choice corresponds to the parties' expectations since they deliberately refrained from agreeing on the law governing their contract, apparently on the assumption that should the question of the applicable law ever arise, the eventually chosen law would protect their interest in a way that any normal business man would consider adequate and reasonable, avoiding any surprises that could result from the application of domestic laws of which they had no deeper knowledge. The particularity of this case—which concerns an agreement on technology exchange and technical cooperation and not a sale of goods—is that the national law was applied only where the Unidroit Principles do not provide an answer to a question of substantive nature raised in the arbitration. This national law was the law of the place of the arbitration, considered as neutral law.[83]

Moreover, the Unidroit Principles have a broader scope than most of their competitors. In every new revision, their scope increases so as to cover the main issues related to long-term contracts.

Finally, the Unidroit Principles contain no rules based on specific regulatory policies[84] but instead recognize the competence of domestic mandatory rules. Indeed, regulatory policies come in from national laws through the opening clauses of Articles 1.4 and 3.3.1. According to Article 1.4, domestic mandatory rules remain applicable, and according to Article 3.3.1, the consequences of a breach of these rules must be derived from this law. This articulation with national mandatory rules increases the effectiveness of the Unidroit Principles since it converges to the traditional limits fixed by any conflict of law rules providing the

---

[82]As an example, the 1999 ICC Award has justified the application of the Unidroit Principles with these arguments: (1) developed by a group of leading international experts, they are an international formulation of general principles applicable to international commercial contracts; (2) they are largely inspired by the CISG which already enjoys international recognition and is generally considered to reflect the customs and practices of international trade in the field of international sale of goods; (3) they are particularly suited to the subject of arbitration; and (4) they consist mainly of clear rules, clearly articulated and organized in a coherent and systematic manner (Award ICC n° 7110 (1998), 54–57).

[83]Arbitration Institute of the Stockholm Chamber of Commerce n° 117/1999 (2001). http://www.unilex.info/case.cfm?id=793. Accessed in 16 June 2016.

[84]For an author: "This dual decision – to not address regulatory policies within the PICC and to refer to domestic laws for them – is wise. It reflects the fact that the PICC – like the ius commune – lack the democratic legitimacy that would be needed for such policy choices." (Michaels (2014), p. 660).

parties' autonomy, such as Article 9 of the 2012 Chinese SPC's opinion or Article 3, paragraphs 3 and 4, and Article 9 of Rome I Regulation.

Although the Unidroit Principles present real advantages with regard to other soft law instruments, their role should continue very residually in the Sino-European contracts of sale of goods, at least in the near future.

2.2 *Residual Role of Unidroit Principles in the Near Future*

The understanding of the actual use of the Unidroit Principles in the international trade, basically as a background law (Sect. 2.2.1), leads us to doubt whether there will be an increase of their use in the Sino-European sale of goods contracts (Sect. 2.2.2).

2.2.1 Unidroit Principles as a Background Law

In Sino-European trade or elsewhere, parties rarely choose the Unidroit Principles. Notwithstanding, adjudicators can use them even if they have not been chosen—be it in situations where the parties referred to the *lex mercatoria* or general customs or, more frequently, in the absence of a party choice. By far, the majority of decisions are those in which the Unidroit Principles are used for interpretation and supplementation of international law and, even more frequently, of domestic law. Furthermore, the Unidroit Principles are increasingly used as custom or international trade usage, which is, at first sight, surprising. Technically, the Unidroit Principles are not a restatement of such usages.[85] They draw, to a large extent, on official law and represent a universal restatement, whereas trade usage is typically unofficial and specific to a particular trade.[86]

Additionally, the use of the Unidroit Principles as a system is rare. Although the Unidroit Principles where drafted as a relatively comprehensive codification, most use is made of individual provisions and in connection with other laws. This is particularly the case where the Unidroit Principles intervene, playing a supplementary role. In such cases, a provision of the Unidroit Principles is not applied or consulted because it is part of the generally applicable law or since such reference to the Unidroit Principles is generally expected. Otherwise, individual provisions are referred to because they seem of particular relevance or usefulness. Indeed, whereas a considerable number of provisions of the Unidroit Principles seem to have never been used, other provisions find repeated use—be it because the provision invoked represents *a restatement of generally accepted rules* or because of its superior quality.[87]

---

[85] Award ICC n° 9029 (1998), 91.

[86] Michaels (2014), p. 649.

[87] Michaels (2014), p. 655.

Definitely, the Unidroit Principles serve more as a reservoir for solutions than a legal order. It means that they serve more as an *objective law* than as an *object of choice*. They are used more by officials—judges and legislators—than by private parties or in privatized adjudication. They are not treated as a code, and much lesser as a legal system, but instead as a compendium of individual provisions, in combination with other legal texts.[88]

Therefore, like *ius commune*, the Unidroit Principles serve, for the time being, as a global background law.[89] The role of a background law is far from unimportant. A background law serves as residual law—it applies if and insofar as the foreground law does not provide an answer. But this is not its only role. In addition, a background law provides the background against which foreground law is interpreted. Since foreground law cannot be interpreted on its own terms, it must be understood in contrast with the background law. Moreover, a properly understood background law "provides the framework within which foreground law functions—it structures, so to speak, its language and its grammar."[90]

2.2.2 A Continuing Modest Role in Sino-European Sale of Goods Contracts

The Sino-European contracts of sale of goods concern a group of international contracts for which a uniform contract law seems absolutely necessary. This is the case since the parties speak different languages and come from countries with big differences between their business culture and their legal systems. If a party does not have the economic power to impose its own law upon the other party, they will most probably agree to a third national law as a neutral one.[91]

Because such a choice is a source of important difficulties related notably to the language, to the certainty of the content of the chosen law, and to the predictability of the outcome of the case under the chosen law,[92] the usefulness or the necessity of using a uniform law to govern international sale of goods between Sino-European companies should not be questioned.

As for the CISG, Unidroit Principles may serve as a tool to bridge cultural differences, offering a neutral and well-adapted law to govern international sale of goods. For these reasons, UNCITRAL formally endorsed the Unidroit Principles at its 40th Plenary Session in 2007 and recommended their use by the international

---

[88]Michaels (2014), p. 657.

[89]Michaels (2014), p. 659.

[90]Michaels (2014), p. 659.

[91]Schwenzer (2016), p. 62.

[92]Schwenzer (2016), pp. 62–64.

business community. In this sense, many international arbitration centers offer tailored choice of law model clauses.[93]

In order to meet these requirements and expectations, and take into account the actual use of the Unidroit Principles in the international trade, three roles the Unidroit Principles could play in the Sino-European contracts of sale of goods should be envisaged.

As Applicable Law Chosen by the Party From a point of view of litigation, parties rarely attempt to choose the Unidroit Principles in contracts before State courts, given the almost unanimous unwillingness of State courts to enforce such a choice. If the Chinese law has recently eliminated such an obstacle, in Europe the Unidroit Principles remain, for litigation, not available as *Law* in the sense of private international law.

The difference of acceptance at the conflict of law level does not contribute to increase the Unidroit Principle as the *lex contractus* since the effectiveness of such a choice will depend on the court before which the litigation will be brought.

Furthermore, even where such a choice may be enforced—in arbitration or before Chinese courts—still the parties need to be convinced of the pertinence of choosing the Unidroit Principles. Indeed, some authors see the parties' lack of interest as an indication that the Unidroit Principles are simply not a good choice.[94]

The arbitral decisions mentioned above confirm somehow this prognostic. An eventual change towards an exclusive choice of Unidroit Principles as *lex contractus* in Sino-European trade remains to be seen.

As Applicable Law in the Absence of Choice Despite paragraph 4 of the Preamble of the Unidroit Principles stating that they may be applied when the parties have not chosen any law to govern their contract, such a role is excluded in current private international law in China, as well as in Europe. Indeed, neither the new Chinese conflict of law rules nor Rome I Convention allow for the application of the Unidroit Principles as an objective contract law. None of them contains a similar rule to Article 9(2)(2) of the 2004 Mexico Convention, which permits the judge to

---

[93]Multilingual model clauses for use by parties of the Unidroit Principles have been suggested, as for example, by the Unidroit (http://www.unidroit.org/instruments/commercial-contracts/upicc-model-clauses), the French ICC and the Chinese European Arbitration Centre in Hamburg (http://www.ceac-arbitration.com/index.php?id=47; see, Brödermann (2011), pp. 593–604. About the promotion of choice of law model clauses by the ICC, see Cuniberti (2016), pp. 774–780.

[94]Michaels (2014), p. 663: "They are not a full codification, much less a legal order; they are 'rules of law,' not 'law'. Even within their area, the law of contracts, they are incomplete in two important regards. First, the Unidroit Principles contain no rules on specific contracts. They are like the PECL and the Common European Sales Law (CESL), confined to rules of general contract law. Second, the Unidroit Principles contain opening clauses for the entry of State national law—be it in presence of mandatory rules (Articles 1.4 and 3.3.1) or gaps (Article 1.6, comment 4). This means, on the one hand, that the parties will not be able to select, in the Unidroit Principles, rules catered specifically to their specific contracts. And it means, on the other hand, that precisely those rules they most want to avoid through their choice remain applicable. With these restrictions, the Unidroit Principles, as chosen law, can have only a supplementary character."

apply, in the absence of a choice, the Unidroit Principles as residual law, that is, as general principles of international commercial law recognized by international organizations. Thus, before the courts, the Unidroit Principles will not be applied as residual applicable law in the absence of choice.

The situation is different in worldwide arbitration, where such an application is largely admitted through the *voie directe* and has influenced the introduction of such a goal into the Preamble of the Unidroit Principles in 2004. However, the application of the Unidroit Principles in the absence of a party's choice remains uncertain in arbitrations under the auspices of CIETAC and other Chinese arbitration commission, even in situations where the arbitrators are faced with one of the parties' request at the beginning of the arbitration. According to Pr. Manjiao, the different grounds pointed out by the reported decisions show that the arbitrators, who must decide in accordance with law, follow the prescribed conflict of law rules to identify the applicable law in the absence of choice. Indeed, since the Unidroit Principles are qualified as "international practice" in Chinese arbitration tribunals, they play a very residual role as provided by Article 142 of the 1986 General Principles of Civil Law and Article 49, paragraph 1 of the Arbitration Rule of CIETAC, as amended in 2014.[95]

Thus, only in arbitrations held by ICC or by other western arbitration tribunals may the application of the Unidroit Principles by the arbitrator, in the absence of party choice, be really expected.

However, the role of the Unidroit Principles is that of a background law whose rules are used individually. Indeed, what we see in practice is that even if arbitrators apply the Unidroit Principles, they rarely do so to the exclusion of other laws. Thus, when they are applicable, they apply as individual rules, not as a whole legal order.

This being said, it is less a matter of application in the sense of paragraph 4 of the Unidroit Principles' Preamble and more of construction and supplementation in the sense of its paragraph 5, according to which "they may be used to interpret or supplement international uniform law instruments." This leads to a last role they might play.

Applicability of the Unidroit Principles to Interpret the CISG The question whether the Unidroit Principles can be used to interpret the CISG or other international conventions is controversial.[96] Against such use, two arguments are dispensed. The first is the suggestion that the CISG must, according to its Article 7(1), be interpreted autonomously, which means be interpreted without reference to one

---

[95] Article 49 Making of Award: "1. The arbitral tribunal shall independently and impartially render a fair and reasonable arbitral award based on the facts of the case and the terms of the contract, in accordance with the law, and with reference to international practices. 2. Where the parties have agreed on the law applicable to the merits of their dispute, the parties' agreement shall prevail. In the absence of such an agreement or where such agreement is in conflict with a mandatory provision of the law, the arbitral tribunal shall determine the law applicable to the merits of the dispute".

[96] On this conroversy, see Schlechtriem and Witz (2008), p. 66.

particular legal system. The second argument is that the Unidroit Principles cannot be the "Principles underlying the CISG," as referenced in Article 7(2) of the CISG, because they did not exist when the CISG was drafted.

According to Pr. Ralf Michaels, these arguments are subject to criticism. With regard to the first, "*obviously, it does not rule out the use of other materials, such as judicial and scholarly opinions. And for the same reason, it cannot mean that the use of a text such as the* [Unidroit Principles] *is ruled out, which serves similar purposes.*" Insofar as the second argument is concerned, "*[w]hat did exist then, however, were general principles of contract law. And to the extent that the* [Unidroit Principles] *restate these general principles, it is unproblematic to view them as the principles in Article 7(2).*"[97]

Following his considerations, it does not mean, however, that the Unidroit Principles can be used in their entirety. Instead, they become a repertory of possible solutions, and their use for interpretation of the CISG must be determined provision by provision. This is particularly the case when they do restate common principles of general contract law. Examples include the calculation of damages in Articles 7.4.2—full compensation[98]—and 7.4.3[99]—certainty of harm—and the definition of standard terms in Article 2.1.19[100] of the Unidroit Principles. At the same time, because Unidroit Principles formulate rules of general contract law, some of their rules are not well suited to the CISG, such as the provision on hardship (Articles 6.2.2 and 6.2.3), which are useful for long-term contracts and changed circumstances. By contrast, the typical sales contract, as governed by the CISG, is a one-off transaction that would be severely impaired if it stood under a general hardship exception.[101]

Notwithstanding the relevance of this approach based on the adaptability of the Unidroit Principles to the CISG issues, to know where the line will be drawn in any particular case can be quite difficult, even if each national jurisdiction and each arbitral tribunal may define it autonomously. The already quoted CIETAC award held in 2004 is a good example.

---

[97] Michaels (2014), pp. 665–666.

[98] Article 7.4.2: "(1) The aggrieved party is entitled to full compensation for harm sustained as a result of the non-performance. Such harm includes both any loss which it suffered and any gain of which it was deprived, taking into account any gain to the aggrieved party resulting from its avoidance of cost or harm. (2) Such harm may be non-pecuniary and includes, for instance, physical suffering or emotional distress."

[99] Article 7.4.3: "(1) Compensation is due only for harm, including future harm, that is established with a reasonable degree of certainty. (2) Compensation may be due for the loss of a chance in proportion to the probability of its occurrence. (3) Where the amount of damages cannot be established with a sufficient degree of certainty, the assessment is at the discretion of the court."

[100] Article 2.1.19: "(1) Where one party or both parties use standard terms in concluding a contract, the general rules on formation apply, subject to Articles 2.1.20–2.1.22. (2) Standard terms are provisions which are prepared in advance for general and repeated use by one party and which are actually used without negotiation with the other party."

[101] Michaels (2014), pp. 666–667.

3 Conclusion

To conclude, even if the new Chinese conflict of rule system creates new possibilities for the parties to choose the Unidroit Principles as applicable law to their contracts, it does not seem exaggerated to say that the Unidroit Principles will continue to play a very residual role in the Sino-European contracts of sale of goods in the near future. More precisely, and as it was already predicted in general terms for all other contracts,[102] the Unidroit Principles shall not become "the" applicable law but rather one of the several bodies of legal rules on which adjudicators draw—no more but also no less.

References

Agrò EF (2011) The impact of the UNIDROIT principles in international. Dispute resolution in figures. Unif Law Rev 16(3):719–733

Barbier H (2016) Les grands mouvement du droit commun des contrats après l'ordonnance du 10 février 2016. RTD civ 6(2):247–262

Brödermann E (2011) The impact of the UNIDROIT principles on international contract and arbitration practice – the experience of a German lawyer. Unif Law Rev 16(3):589–612

Brödermann E (2012) 1. Teil, Grundlagen des Internationalen Privatrechts. In: Brödermann E, Rosengarten J (eds) Internationales Privat- und Verfahrensrecht (IPR/IZVR) (on European and German private international law and international procedural law), 6th edn. Verlag Franz Vahlen, München

Bonell MJ (2001) Do we need a global commercial code ? Dickinson Law Rev 106:87–100

Bonell MJ (2005a) Soft law and party autonomy: the case of the UNIDROIT principles. Loy L Rev 51:229–252

Bonell JM (2005b) An international restatement of contract law: the UNIDROIT principles of international commercial contracts, 3rd edn. Transnational Publishers, Inc., Irvington, New York

Cavalieri Renzo R, Franzina P (eds) (2012) Il nuovo diritto internazionale privato della Repubblica Popolare Cinese. La legge del 28 ottobre 2010 sul diritto applicabile ai rapporti civili con elementi di estraneita'. Giuffrè Ed., Milano

Cerqueira G (2011) O novo Direito Internacional Privado chinês – Aspectos gerais e contratuais a propósito da nova Lei da República popular da China, de 28 de outubro de 2010. Revista dos Tribunais 906:181–228

Cerqueira G, Nord N, Porcheron D (2011) Les nouvelles règles de conflit de lois chinoises en matière contractuelle. Rev Lamy dr aff 61:52–56

Chen W, Bertrand L (2011) La nouvelle loi chinoise de droit international privé du 28 octobre 2010: contexte législatif, principales nouveautés et critiques. JDI (Clunet) 2:375–389

Cuniberti G (2016) La *lex mercatoria* au XXIe Une analyse empirique et économique. JDI (Clunet) 3:765–780

Dennis MJ (2014) Modernizing and harmonizing international contract law: the CISG and the UNIDROIT principles continue to provide the best way forward. Unif Law Rev 19(1):114–151

[102]Michaels (2014), p. 647 and ff.

Derains Y (2002) The role of the Unidroit principles in international commercial arbitration (1): a European perspective. In: ICC, UNIDROIT Principles of International Commercial Contracts. ICC Bulletin Special Supplement, pp 9–20
Estrella Faria JA (2016) The influence of the UNIDROIT principles of international commercial contracts on national laws. Unif Law Rev 21:238–270
Fauvarque-Cosson B (2014) Le droit international privé des contrats en Marche vers l'universalité. In: d'Avout, L Bureau, D Muir-Watt, H (eds) Les relations privées internationales. Mélanges en l'honneur du professeur Bernard Audit. LGDJ, Paris, pp 269–284
Fauvarque-Cosson B, Mazeaud D (coord.), Tenebaum A (dir.) (2008a) Terminologie ccontractuelle commune. Association Henri Capitant des Amis de la Culture Juridique Française et Société de Législation Comparée, Projet de Cadre commun de référence. SLC, Paris
Fauvarque-Cosson B, Mazeaud D (coord), Wicker G, Racine JB (dir) (2008b). Principes contractuels communs. Association Henri Capitant des Amis de la culture Juridique Française et Société de Législation Comparée, Projet de Cadre commun de référence. SLC, Paris
Gabriel HD (2013) Unidroit principles as a source for global sales law. Vill L Rev 58(4):661–680
Goldman B (1963) Le droit des sociétés internationales. JDI (Clunet) 1:320–388
Han S (2013) Principles of Asian contract law: an endeavor of regional harmonization of contract law in East Asia. Vill L Rev 58(4):589–599
Huang J (2008) Direct application of international commercial law in Chinese courts: intellectual property, trade, and international transportation. Manchester J Int Econ Law 105(5):105–142
Huo Z (2011) An imperfect improvement: the new conflict of Laws act of the People's republic of China. ICLQ 60(4):1063–1093
Lando O (2005) CISG and its followers: a proposal to adopt some international principles of contract law. Am J Comp L Law 53(2):379–401
Lando O, Beale H (eds) (1999) Principles of European contract law, parts I and II. Kluwer Law International, The Hague, London, Boston
Lando O, Clive E, Prüm A, Zimmermann R (eds) (2003) Principles on European contract law, Part III. Kluwer Law International, The Hague, London, Boston
Lefebvre G, Jiao J (2002) Les principes d'Unidroit et le droit chinois: convergences et dissonances. In: Les Principes d'Unidroit et les contrats internationaux: aspects pratiques. Thémis, Montréal, pp 139–150
Li-Kotovtchikhine XY (2002) Le nouveau droit chinois des contrats internationaux. JDI (Clunet) 1:113–163
Manjiao C (2010) Application of the UNIDROIT principles in China: successes, shortcomings and implications. Unif Law Rev 15(1):5–36
Michaels R (2014) The Unidroit principles as global background law. Unif Law Rev 19 (4):643–668
Nord N, Cerqueira G (2011) Comments on the Chinese new statute on conflict os laws: a European perspective. Chin Yearb Private Int Law Comp Law 14:70–101
Nord N, Cerqueira G (2016) La codification de la résolution du conflit de lois en Chine et son interprétation par la Cour suprême: entre progrés et incertitudes. JDI (Clunet) 1:79–104
Pissler KB (2012) Das neue internationale Privatrecht der Volksrepublik China: Nach den Steinen tastend den Fluss überqueren. RabelsZ 76:1–46
Ramberg J (2013) Cisg and UPICC as the basis for an international convention on international commercial contracts. Vill L Rev 58(4):681–690
Rapport au Président de la République relatif à l'ordonnance n° 2016-131 du 10 février 2016 portant réforme du droit des contrats, du régime général et de la preuve des obligations, JORF n° 0035 du 11 février 2016, Texte n° 25
Schlechtriem P, Witz C (2008) Convention de Vienne sur les contrats de vente internationale de marchandises. Dalloz, Paris
Seraglini C (2003) Du bon usage des principes UNIDROIT dans l'arbitrage international. Revue de l'Arbitrage 4:1101–1166

Shaohui Z (2003) L'internationalisation du nouveau droit chinois des contrats : exemple de la résolution du contrat de vente internationale de marchandises. Unif Law Rev 1-2(8):219–230
Shaohui Z (2008) L'influence des Principes d'UNIDROIT sur la réforme du droit chinois des obligations. Unif Law Rev 1-2(13):153–178
Schwenzer I (2016) Global unification of contract law. Unif L Rev 21:60–74
Tu G (2011) China's new conflicts code : general issues and selected topics. Am J Comp Law 59 (2):563–590
Von Bar C, Clive E, Schulte-Nölke H (eds) (2008) Principles, Definitions and model rules of European private law: draft common frame of reference. Interim Outline Edition. Sellier, München
Xiao Y, Long W (2009) Contractual party autonomy in Chinese private international law. Yearb Private Int Law 11:193–209
Zhang Y, Huang D (2000) The new contract law in the People's Republic of China and the UNIDROIT principles of international commercial contracts: a brief comparison. Unif Law Rev 3(5):429–440

Judicial Decisions and Arbitral Awards

Cass. ch. civ., sect. civ., 21 juin 1950, *Messageries maritimes*, Rev. crit. DIP 1950. 609, note Batiffol, D. 1951. 749, note Hamel, S. 1952. 1. 1, note Niboyet, J.C.P. 1950. II. 5812, note J. Ph. Lévy.
Cass. civ., 6 mars 1876, *Canal de Capronne*, D. 76. 1. 193, note Giboulot.
Cass. com., 17 février 2015, n° 12-29.550, 13-18.956, 13-20.230, non publié au Bulletin.
Tribunal Supremo, Case n° 74/2012 (29 February 2012). http://www.unilex.info/case.cfm?id=1652. Accessed 11 June 2016.
Award ICC n° 9474 (2001), ICC International Court of Arbitration Bulletin, Vol. 12, No. 2 (Fall 2001), 60-67.
Award ICC n° 10114 (2000). ICC International Court of Arbitration Bulletin, Vol. 12, No 2 (Fall 2001), 82-84.
Award ICC n° 7110 (1998), ICC International Court of Arbitration Bulletin, Vol. 10, No. 2, Fall 1999, 54-57.
Award ICC n° 9029 (1998), ICC International Court of Arbitration Bulletin, Vol. 10, No. 2, Fall 1999, 88-96.
Award ICC n° 7375 (1996), Measley's International Arbitration Report, 1996, 11: A-1 A-69.
International Arbitration Court of the Chamber of Commerce and Industry of the Russian Federation, 16 July 2013, n° 177/2012. http://www.unilex.info/case.cfm?id=1807. Accessed in 11 June 2016.
International Arbitration Court of the Chamber of Commerce and Industry of the Russian Federation, 27 May 2013, n° 166/2012. http://www.unilex.info/case.cfm?id=1791. Accessed in 11 June 2016.
International Arbitration Court of the Chamber of Commerce and Industry of the Russian Federation, 2 June 2009, n° 148. http://www.unilex.info/case.cfm?id=1552. Accessed in 11 June 2016.
China International Economic and Trade Arbitration Commission, unknown date (2007). http://www.unilex.info/case.cfm?id=1208. Accessed in 14 juin 2016.
Shaoguan Intermediate People's Court, 28 April 2005, *Hengxing Company v. Guangdong Petrochemical Subsidiary Company*. An abstract of this case is available at http://www.unilex.info/case.cfm?id=1120. Accessed in 11 June 2016.
China International Economic and Trade Arbitration Commission, 2 September 2005. http://www.unilex.info/case.cfm?id=1355. Accessed in 14 juin 2016.

China International Economic and Trade Arbitration Commission, September 2004, n° 0291-1: http://www.unilex.info/case.cfm?id=1441. Accessed in 14 juin 2016.

Arbitration Institute of the Stockholm Chamber of Commerce, 2001, n° 117/1999. http://www.unilex.info/case.cfm?id=793. Accessed in 16 June 2016.

Online Documents

Chinese European Arbitration Centre in Hamburg - Choice of Law Clause: (http://www.ceac-arbitration.com/index.php?id=47, Accessed 7 November 2016.

Gandolfi G (2001) The Academy of European Private Lawyers and the Pavia Draft of a "European Contract Code"'. http://ec.europa.eu/consumers/cons_int/safe_shop/fair_bus_pract/cont_law/stake) and the Trento Common Core Project (see <www.common-core.org/). Accessed 18 June 2016.

Model Clauses for Use by Parties of the UNIDROIT Principles of International Commercial Contracts: http://www.unidroit.org/instruments/commercial-contracts/upicc-model-clauses), Accessed 7 November 2016.

Réforme du droit des contrats: 3 questions à Carole Champalaune (Directrice des affaires civiles et du Sceau): http://www.textes.justice.gouv.fr/dossiers-thematiques-10083/loi-du-170215-sur-la-simplification-du-droit-12766/reforme-du-droit-des-contrats-3-questions-a-carole-champalaune-27931.html. Accessed 10 June 2016.

UNCITRAL, Possible Future Work in the Area of International Contract Law: Proposal by Switzerland on Possible Future Work by UNCITRAL in the Area of International Contract Law, 45th session, New York, 25 June–6 July 2012, Doc A/CN.9/758 (8 May 2012). http://www.uncitral.org/uncitral/commission/sessions/45th.html. Accessed 10 June 2016.

World Trade Organization, World Trade Statistical Review 2016, Merchandise trade and trade in commercial services. https://www.wto.org/english/res_e/statis_e/wts2016_e/WTO_Chapter_04_e.pdf. Accessed 7 November 2016.

World Trade Organization, World Trade Statistical Review 2016, Statistical table. https://www.wto.org/english/res_e/statis_e/wts2016_e/WTO_Chapter_09_tables_e.pdf. Accessed 7 November 2016.

Part IV
International Sale of Goods and Consumers

International Consumer Sales: International Jurisdiction and ADR in Europe and China

Markus Petsche

1 Introduction

Consumer protection constitutes a major policy objective in both the European Union (EU)[1] (and its Member States taken individually) and China.[2] Adequate protection of consumers requires the adoption of specific legislation in a variety of substantive and procedural (i.e., dispute resolution) areas. This chapter focuses on the latter aspect and deals with two particular issues relevant to international consumer transactions: (a) rules on international jurisdiction over consumer disputes and (b) the use, availability, and functioning of ADR procedures to resolve such disputes.

Section 1 of this chapter explores the international jurisdiction of EU and Chinese courts over international consumer disputes. It notably examines whether, and to what extent, the European and Chinese legislators have adopted preferential jurisdictional rules specific to consumer disputes. Of particular practical relevance in this context are the questions of whether (a) consumers enjoy the right to sue traders in their (i.e., the consumers') home courts, (b) whether there are limitations on the rights of traders to sue consumers in courts other than their (i.e., the consumers') home courts, and (c) whether there are any restrictions on the validity and/or enforceability of choice-of-court and arbitration agreements that would derogate from the applicable preferential jurisdictional rules, if any.

[1]See Sempi (2011), pp. 4–8.

[2]As early as 1993, the Chinese legislator adopted the "Law of the People's Republic of China on Protection of Consumer Rights and Interests". The law was substantially revised in 2013. For a critical analysis of those revisions, see Zhixiong (2014).

M. Petsche (✉)
Central European University, Budapest, Hungary
e-mail: PetscheM@ceu.edu

N. Nord, G. Cerqueira (eds.), *International Sale of Goods*, China-EU Law Series 5,
DOI 10.1007/978-3-319-54036-8_9

Section 2 examines the use of ADR to resolve (international) consumer disputes. In this context, ADR must be understood in a broad sense to include not only nonbinding procedures such as mediation, conciliation, and the like but also binding procedures such as arbitration. Section 2 provides an overview of the current practice of consumer ADR and discusses recent legislative enactments aimed at promoting recourse to such alternative processes. It also examines the availability of ODR (online dispute resolution) mechanisms as a tool to settle disputes arising from transactions concluded online.

2 International Jurisdiction

2.1 International Jurisdiction of European Courts

2.1.1 Legal Framework: Brussels I Regulation (Recast)

Brussels I Regulation (recast) (formally entitled "Regulation (EU) No 1215/2012 of the European Parliament and of the Council of 12 December 2012 on jurisdiction and recognition and enforcement of judgments in civil and commercial matters") constitutes the revised version of a 2001 Regulation carrying the same name, which, in turn, resulted from the incorporation into EU law of the 1968 Brussels Convention.[3] In addition to rules governing the recognition and enforcement of judgments, the Regulation lays down jurisdictional rules common to the Member States of the EU.[4] It is, by definition, only concerned with determining the jurisdiction of the courts of EU Member States and not of foreign (non-EU) courts.

The scope of application of the Regulation is the subject of a twofold limitation. First of all, as its title suggests, the Regulation only applies to "civil and commercial matters." It does not, therefore, apply to "revenue, customs or administrative matters or to the liability of the State for acts and omissions in the exercise of State authority."[5] In addition, several categories of civil and commercial disputes are expressly excluded from its scope under Article 1(2) of the Regulation.

Second, in principle, the Regulation's jurisdictional rules only apply to disputes involving a defendant domiciled in the EU.[6] In other words, if the defendant is domiciled in China or the United States, for example, the Regulation does not in principle apply. In such cases, the jurisdiction of the courts of a particular Member State has to be determined on the basis of the relevant domestic rules on

[3]Convention on jurisdiction and the enforcement of judgments in civil and commercial matters of 27 September 1968.

[4]It has to be noted, however, that the Regulation does not apply in or to Denmark. See Recital 41 of the Regulation's Preamble.

[5]Regulation Art. 1(1).

[6]See Recital 14 of the Regulation's Preamble.

jurisdiction.[7] However, in exceptional cases, the Regulation's jurisdictional rules may apply even where the defendant is domiciled *outside* the EU. As shall be seen below, disputes arising from consumer contracts are one such exception.

2.1.2 Overview of Jurisdictional Rules

The Regulation sets forth a basic jurisdictional principle, as well as a number of more specific jurisdictional rules. The former consists of the rule according to which a defendant may be sued in the courts of the country of his domicile.[8] The latter include rules of "special jurisdiction"[9] (notably rules specific to contract and tort claims), rules pertaining to particular categories of contracts (insurance,[10] consumer,[11] and employment contracts[12]), rules of exclusive jurisdiction,[13] and rules related to "prorogation of jurisdiction."[14]

2.1.3 Specific Rules Applying to Consumer Transactions

The Regulation lays down rules specific to consumer transactions in Articles 17 to 19. Article 17 delineates the scope of application of these specific rules, notably by defining the crucial concept of "consumer contract." Article 18 sets forth the applicable (default) jurisdictional rules (see Sects. 2.1.4 and 2.1.5 below), while Article 19 deals with the validity of agreements derogating from those jurisdictional rules (see Sect. 2.1.6 below).

The material scope of the consumer-specific jurisdictional rules contained in Articles 18 and 19 is defined by reference to two criteria. Firstly, and evidently, those specific rules only apply to transactions entered into by *consumers*, i.e., to contracts "concluded by a person... for a purpose which can be regarded as being outside his trade or profession."[15] Secondly, the relevant rules only apply to specific *forms* or *categories* of such consumer transactions, namely, (a) contracts for the sale of goods on installment credit terms, (b) loan contracts and other contracts entered into to finance the purchase of goods, and, (c) more generally, all contracts

[7]See Regulation Art. 6(1): "If the defendant is not domiciled in a Member State, the jurisdiction of the courts of each Member State shall... be determined by the law of that Member State."

[8]See Regulation Art. 4(1): "Subject to this Regulation, persons domiciled in a Member State shall, whatever their nationality, be sued in the courts of that Member State."

[9]Regulation Art. 7–9.

[10]Regulation Art. 10–16.

[11]Regulation Art. 17–19.

[12]Regulation Art. 20–23.

[13]Regulation Art. 24.

[14]Regulation Art. 25–26.

[15]Regulation Art. 17(1).

concluded with a person who pursues commercial of professional activities in the Member State of the consumer's domicile or who directs such activities to that Member State.[16]

2.1.4 Where Can Consumers Sue?

Under Article 18(1), consumers may bring claims either in the courts of the trader's domicile or in the courts of their own domicile (i.e., the consumers' domicile). A French consumer may, for example, sue a German trader in either the German (courts of the trader's domicile) or the French courts (courts of the consumer's domicile). Article 18(1) therefore grants consumers a jurisdictional "privilege," effectively protecting them from the risk of having to litigate in a foreign country.

In derogation from the general rule according to which the Regulation only applies where the defendant is domiciled in the EU, the jurisdictional privilege contained in Article 18(1) also applies where the defendant is not domiciled in the EU (it applies "regardless of the domicile of the other party"). This means that a French or German consumer, for example, may sue a Chinese trader in the French or German courts respectively.

2.1.5 Where Can Consumers Be Sued?

In order adequately to protect consumers from the risk of having to litigate abroad, jurisdictional rules must prevent professionals from suing consumers in courts other than those of their (i.e., the consumers') domicile. Such protection is achieved by Article 18(2) of the Regulation, according to which "[p]roceedings may be brought against a consumer ... only in the courts of the Member State in which the consumer is domiciled." Accordingly, a French consumer, for example, may only be sued in the competent French courts. It has to be noted in this respect that Article 18(2) only applies to the jurisdiction of EU courts and that it does not, and cannot, prevent non-EU courts from affirming jurisdiction over claims brought against EU (e.g., French) consumers.

2.1.6 Validity of Choice-of-Court and Arbitration Agreements

The protection afforded to consumers under the jurisdictional rules of Article 18 would be ineffective if those rules could be (easily) derogated from by the parties. Two types of agreements may have such a derogative effect: (a) choice-of-court agreements and (b) arbitration agreements.

---

[16]Regulation Art. 17(1).

As far as choice-of-court agreements are concerned, the Regulation restricts their validity to three categories of such agreements: (a) those that are entered into after the dispute has arisen (because it can be assumed that such agreements are freely entered into by the consumer), (b) those that offer additional jurisdictional options to the consumer (without affecting the consumer's ability to bring claims before the courts having jurisdiction under Article 18), and (c) those that provide for the jurisdiction of the courts of the parties' common domicile at the time of the conclusion of the contract (this rule applies to cases where either the consumer or the other party's domicile is no longer in the same country at the time when the dispute arises).[17]

As regards arbitration agreements, it has to be noted that the Regulation excludes arbitration from its scope.[18] However, arbitration agreements arguably fall within the scope of the Regulation's broad concept of "provisions [which] depart[...] from" Article 18's jurisdictional rules.[19] In any event, under the Directive on unfair terms in consumer contracts of April 5, 1993, arbitration clauses contained in consumer contracts are, in principle, void. In fact, under the Directive, such clauses are regarded as unfair,[20] i.e., as causing "a significant imbalance in the parties' rights and obligations ... to the detriment of the consumer."[21]

2.2 *International Jurisdiction of Chinese Courts*

2.2.1 Legal Framework

The rules pertaining to the international jurisdiction of Chinese courts can be found in the Civil Procedure Law (CPL) of the People's Republic of China. This law, which was adopted in 1991 and revised in 2007 and 2012 respectively, constitutes a comprehensive codification of principles of civil procedure. Of particular relevance for present purposes is Part 4 of the law, which is entitled "Special Provisions of the Civil Procedures Involving Foreign Elements." Chapter 24, which is contained in

---

[17]Regulation Art. 19.

[18]Regulation Art. 1(2)(d).

[19]Regulation Art. 19.

[20]The Directive's Annex contains an indicative and non-exhaustive list of terms which may be regarded as unfair. Section 1(q) of that Annex refers to terms which have the object or effect of "excluding or hindering the consumer's right to take legal action or exercise any other legal remedy, particularly by requiring the consumer to take disputes exclusively to arbitration not covered by legal provisions, unduly restricting the evidence available to him or imposing on him a burden of proof which, according to the applicable law, should lie with another party to the contract."

[21]See Directive Art. 3(1): "A contractual term which has not been individually negotiated shall be regarded as unfair if, contrary to the requirement of good faith, it causes a significant imbalance in the parties' rights and obligations arising under the contract, to the detriment of the consumer."

Part 4, deals with jurisdiction. It contains two provisions (Articles 265 and 266), only the first one being relevant in the context of consumer transactions.

2.2.2 General Jurisdictional Rules

Like the Regulation, the Chinese Civil Procedure Law recognizes the general principle of the jurisdiction of the courts of the defendant's domicile. This principle is expressly adopted in Article 21 CPL, according to which "[a] civil lawsuit brought against a citizen shall be under the jurisdiction of the people's court located in the place where the defendant has his domicile." It can also be found in various other provisions, notably those pertaining to contract[22] and tort[23] claims.

Although Part 4 of the CPL, which is related to disputes "involving foreign elements," does not contain a rule similar to Article 21, courts and scholars agree that the principle of the jurisdiction of the courts of the defendant's domicile should apply by analogy or extension. As Zhenjie points out,[24] Article 259 CPL provides that issues that are not directly addressed in Part 4 should be resolved in reliance on provisions contained in other parts.[25]

In addition to recognizing the general competence of the courts of the defendant's domicile, the CPL also specifies the circumstances under which foreign defendants, i.e., defendants not domiciled in China, may be sued in the Chinese courts. These circumstances comprise the following five scenarios: (a) the place of conclusion or of performance of the contract is in China, (b) the subject matter of the action is located in China, (c) the defendant owns assets in China, (d) the breach of contract occurred in China, and (e) the defendant has a representative branch, agency, or agent in China.[26]

2.2.3 Jurisdiction of Chinese Courts Over Consumer Disputes

Unlike the Regulation, the CPL does not contain any jurisdictional rules specific to consumer disputes. There are two likely explanations for this: Firstly, consumer protection law in China is, for a number of reasons, still much less developed than

[22]CPL Art. 23.

[23]CPL Art. 28.

[24]Zhenjie (1999), p. 207 (observing that "domicile and habitual residence of the defendant are the principal connecting factors of jurisdiction for purely domestic cases as well as for those involving foreign elements").

[25]CPL Art. 259 provides: "The provisions of this Part shall be applicable to any civil litigation involving foreign elements within the territory of the People's Republic of China. Where it is not covered by the provisions of this Part, other relevant provisions of this Law shall apply."

[26]CPL Art. 265. For commentary on these jurisdictional bases, see Zhenjie (1999), pp. 209–222.

in Europe.[27] Secondly, the emphasis of consumer protection in China has so far been placed on substantive, rather than procedural, protections.

Since it does not provide for any consumer-specific jurisdictional rules, the CPL does evidently not grant Chinese consumers a general right to bring proceedings in the Chinese courts. Nor does it protect foreign consumers from the threat of having to litigate in the Chinese courts. To what extent (a) Chinese consumers may initiate proceedings in China and (b) foreign consumers may be sued in China will depend on whether the different jurisdictional requirements set forth in Article 265 are met.

As regards claims brought by Chinese consumers, the Chinese courts will affirm their jurisdiction, notably if (a) the place of conclusion or performance is in China, (b) the professional has assets in China, or (c) the professional has a branch, agency, or agent in China. Of particular relevance in this context may be the determination of the place of performance of the contract, which requires a preliminary determination of the performance that is relevant for establishing jurisdiction. (The consumer's performance? The trader's performance? The breaching party's performance?)

It is noteworthy that Article 265 CPL fails to provide any guidance as to how the relevant place of performance should be determined. It is also interesting to note that under Chinese law, there exists only one place of performance for a particular contract. Unlike in most European jurisdictions, Chinese law does not therefore distinguish between the various obligations that arise under a given contract. In relation to a contract for the sale of goods, for example, the Chinese Supreme Court has held that the place of performance that is relevant for the purposes of establishing jurisdiction is the place of delivery, regardless of whether the claim alleges a violation of the seller's or the buyer's obligations.

The presence of a representative agency, branch, or business agent belonging to, or affiliated with, a foreign trader may also serve as a basis for the jurisdiction of the Chinese courts. The terms "representative agency," "branch," and "business agent" are not defined in the law, and there may be some uncertainty as to the precise meaning of these concepts. One important question that arises in relation to this jurisdictional ground is the question of the scope of jurisdiction, i.e., the question of whether the Chinese courts' jurisdiction is general or limited to the specific activities of the relevant agency, branch, or agent. Scholars have expressed a preference for a more restrictive, functional interpretation.[28]

As far as claims brought against foreign consumers are concerned, the jurisdiction of the Chinese courts will similarly depend on whether the requirements of Article 265 are met. Under this provision, such a risk (from the point of view of the consumer) exists, though its importance should not be exaggerated. Indeed, in the vast majority cases, consumer disputes relate to claims initiated by consumers against traders and not vice versa. Also, a Chinese trader may in any event be

---

[27]See Li and Zhou (2012) (stating that "[w]hen Chinese legislators prepared the draft CCPI [Consumer Protection Law], EU consumer protection law was taken as reference point. However, nearly 20 years after, while the EU has made great progress in the field, China is far behind.").

[28]Zhenjie (1999), p. 213.

dissuaded from initiating proceedings in China in light of the expense and difficulty associated with enforcement of the Chinese court's decision in the consumer's home jurisdiction.

3 ADR as a Mechanism to Settle Consumer Disputes

3.1 *Benefits of ADR*

Empirical data suggest that consumers only very rarely initiate judicial proceedings against professionals. According to a recent study examining consumer disputes in the EU, only 2% of consumers experiencing grievances (i.e., having a reason to initiate proceedings) actually bring a claim before a court.[29] The reasons for this reluctance to resort to the courts are likely to comprise various factors, including (a) the significant (and often disproportionate) time and cost associated with litigation, (b) the complexity of the process, and (c) psychological barriers (such as fear or apprehension) preventing consumers from availing themselves of judicial remedies.[30]

The use of ADR, in particular of nonbinding procedures such as mediation and conciliation, may help to address some or all of these concerns. First of all, ADR procedures such as mediation are generally much faster than litigation and, by way of consequence, considerably less expensive. Second, from the point of view of the consumer, entering into an "amicable" and nonbinding process is a much less frightening prospect than appearing before a judge in a formal court proceeding.

3.2 *Consumer ADR in the EU*

3.2.1 Use of ADR

In the general field of civil and commercial disputes, the use of ADR (to the exception of arbitration) has traditionally been, and remains, limited. The European legislator has made several attempts to promote the use of ADR and, more particularly, of mediation (notably by adopting the 2008 Mediation Directive[31]). However, these attempts have so far been rather unsuccessful.[32]

The use of ADR to resolve *consumer* disputes has also been rather sporadic. Some of the factors accounting for the limited recourse to ADR by consumers

[29]European Commission, Impact Assessment (2011), p. 13.

[30]European Commission, Impact Assessment (2011), p. 13.

[31]Directive 2008/52/EC OF THE EUROPEAN PARLIAMENT AND OF THE COUNCIL of 21 May 2008 on certain aspects of mediation in civil and commercial matters.

[32]European Parliament (2014), "Rebooting" the Mediation Directive.

include (a) lack of awareness of the existence and/or availability of such mechanisms and (b) skepticism as to the usefulness of nonbinding procedures given that their success ultimately depends on the parties' ability to agree on specific settlement terms. Recently adopted instruments (see below Sects. 3.2.2 and 3.2.3) have sought to remedy these defects.

3.2.2 Directive on Consumer ADR

The Directive on Consumer ADR (Directive 2013/11/EU of the European Parliament and of the Council of 21 May 2013 on alternative dispute resolution for consumer disputes) applies to both domestic and cross-border intra-EU consumer disputes,[33] the latter ones being defined as disputes involving a trader and a consumer who are established in different EU Member States.[34] It is noteworthy that, unlike some of the provisions of the Regulation (such as Art. 18(1)), the Directive does not apply to consumer disputes involving traders who are established outside the EU.

The Directive pursues three broad objectives: (a) to improve (consumer) access to ADR, (b) to increase awareness of the availability of ADR processes, and (c) to ensure the quality and efficiency of those processes. As regards the first objective, the Directive obliges Member States to ensure the general availability of ADR "schemes" for all consumer disputes.[35] The concept of ADR scheme refers to the existence of a specific institution or entity (referred to as "ADR entity"[36]) that administers ADR procedures in accordance with specific preestablished rules. Importantly, the procedures administered by these entities must be either free of charge or offered at nominal cost.[37]

Increasing the consumers' awareness of the availability of ADR mechanisms is another important objective pursued by the Directive. Under the Directive, the primary responsibility for ensuring a high degree of awareness lies with the traders. Those traders who are bound by a particular scheme (whether as a result of a statutory obligation or a voluntary undertaking) must inform consumers of the availability of the scheme in question.[38] Such information must be made available on the trader's website (if any) and must also be contained in the general conditions of contract (if any).[39]

---

[33]Directive Art. 2(1).

[34]Directive Art. 2(1).

[35]Art. 5(1) of the Directive provides: "Member States... shall ensure that disputes covered by this Directive and which involve a trader established on their respective territories can be submitted to an ADR entity which complies with the requirements set out in this Directive."

[36]Under Art. 4(1)(h) of the Directive, an ADR entity is defined as "any entity, however named or referred to, which is established on a durable basis and offers the resolution of a dispute through an ADR procedure".

[37]Directive Art. 8(c).

[38]Directive Art. 13(1).

[39]Directive Art. 13(2).

Lastly, several provisions of the Directive aim to ensure the quality and efficiency of the relevant ADR procedures. Some of the most significant rules include (a) various quality requirements applicable to ADR entities, (b) requirements applicable to the individuals in charge of conducting ADR procedures,[40] and (c) various procedural requirements.[41] In addition, the Directive sets a rather strict time limit for the completion of an ADR procedure.[42]

3.2.3 Regulation on Consumer ODR

The Regulation on Consumer ODR (Regulation (EU) No 524/2013 of the European Parliament and of the Council of 21 May 2013 on online dispute resolution for consumer disputes) deals, as its name suggests, with online dispute resolution mechanisms, i.e., mechanisms that are entirely administered online (i.e., via the Internet). The main object and purpose of the Regulation is to establish an ODR platform for processing complaints arising from online consumer transactions. The platform was officially launched on February 15, 2016, and can be accessed at https://webgate.ec.europa.eu/odr/main/index.cfm?event=main.home.chooseLanguage.

Similarly to the ADR Directive, the ODR Regulation applies to both domestic and cross-border intra-EU disputes, i.e., disputes involving a consumer and a trader who are both domiciled or established in the EU.[43] The Regulation does not, therefore, apply to disputes involving traders who are established outside the EU (e.g., US or Chinese traders). The Regulation further specifies that it applies to all disputes arising from online sales and services contracts, thereby covering virtually all forms of online consumer transactions.[44]

The online platform fulfills three principal functions. First of all, both consumers and traders can use the platform in order to file complaints.[45] Second, the administrator of the platform transmits complaints to the other party or parties and to the competent ADR entity, to the extent that the parties are bound to have their dispute settled by a particular entity.[46] Third, the platform also offers the parties a comprehensive electronic case management system.[47]

[40] See, in particular, Art. 6 of the Directive establishing requirements of expertise, independence and impartiality.

[41] See, in particular, Articles 7, 8 and 9 of the Directive respectively related to the transparency, effectiveness, and fairness of ADR procedures.

[42] Article 8(e) of the Directive provides that: "the outcome of the ADR procedure [shall be] made available within a period of 90 calendar days from the date on which the ADR entity has received the complete complaint file."

[43] Regulation Art. 2(1).

[44] Regulation Art. 2(1).

[45] Regulation Art. 8.

[46] Regulation Art. 9.

[47] Regulation Art. 10–11.

3.3 Consumer ADR in China

3.3.1 General Role of ADR

Unlike in the Western world, ADR, and more specifically mediation, has always played an import role in China.[48] This can notably be seen from the fact that so-called judicial mediation, i.e. mediation performed by a judge in the exercise of his/her judicial function, is widely practiced in China. The importance of ADR is further evidenced by the similar practice of "arbitral mediation," which consists of the exercise by an arbitrator of the function of a mediator. More generally, the Chinese legal system and culture do not draw very rigid distinctions between the various methods of dispute settlement but view them more holistically.

3.3.2 Promotion of the Use of ADR in Connection with Consumer Disputes

In recent years, the general preference for ADR has also led to legislative promotion of ADR, notably in relation to consumer disputes. Under Article 39 of the Consumer Protection Law (CPL), consumer disputes may be submitted not only to the competent Chinese courts but also—provided that the parties agree—to mediation by consumer organizations or arbitration. Recently, some Chinese scholars have advocated the creation of a system of mandatory arbitration of consumer disputes to be administered by consumer organizations.[49] Whether such suggestions will be acted upon by the legislator is yet uncertain.

As regards consumer ODR, it is also becoming increasingly popular and widespread in China.[50] Currently available institutions and procedures notably include (a) the Online Dispute Resolution Center established by China's E-Commerce Laws Nets and Beijing Deofar Consulting Ltd., (b) internal complaint mechanisms (such as the one set up by Taobao), and (c) online petition systems created by various nonprofit organizations and consumer protection groups.[51] While there are still obstacles to the efficient functioning of these mechanisms and procedures, there appears to be consensus among businesses, consumer protection organizations, and government agencies that consumer ODR should be further promoted and expanded.[52]

---

[48]See Sempi (2011), p. 11 (referring to the "propensity towards a non-judicial solution of disputes traditionally rooted in East Asian societies).

[49]See Zhixiong (2014), p. 168.

[50]See Xu.

[51]Xu, p. 2.

[52]Xu, pp. 4–6.

4 Conclusion

Rules on international jurisdiction and the promotion of ADR and ODR both perform an important function in the protection of the procedural interests of consumers transacting with foreign traders. Jurisdictional rules are of vital importance to protect consumers from the need to litigate their claims abroad, while the availability of ADR and ODR procedures ensures better access to justice. Indeed, as has been explained, all too often the cost and length of court proceedings discourages consumers from seeking judicial redress.

As regards jurisdictional rules, very different pictures present themselves to the observer in Europe and China. While Brussels I Regulation effectively eliminates any threat for European consumers to have to litigate in a foreign court (within the Regulation's scope), the absence of any specific jurisdictional rules in China leaves the door open to such scenarios. The Chinese legislator may thus consider amending the current Civil Procedure Law accordingly.

As far as ADR and ODR are concerned, both the European and the Chinese legislators are actively promoting their uses in relation to consumer disputes. In both the EU and China, the focus has so far been on domestic or, in the case of the EU, domestic and intra-EU disputes. In Europe, this restricted scope may partly be due to questions of EU competence relative to Member State competences. In any event, one of the big challenges ahead will be the creation of a legal framework going beyond the scope of domestic and intra-EU disputes. Also, and more generally, it remains to be seen to what extent the recent initiatives discussed in this contribution will achieve their objectives, namely a more frequent use by consumers of ADR and ODR procedures.

References

European Commission, COMMISSION STAFF WORKING PAPER, IMPACT ASSESSMENT accompanying the document Proposal for a Directive of the European Parliament and of the Council on Alternative Dispute Resolution for consumer disputes (Directive on consumer ADR) and Proposal for a Regulation of the European Parliament and of the Council on Online Dispute Resolution for consumer disputes (regulation on consumer ODR), SEC(2011) 1408 final, 29 November 2011

European Parliament, Directorate General for Internal Policies, Policy Department C: Citizens' Rights and Constitutional Affairs, Legal Affairs, "Rebooting" the Mediation Directive: Assessing the Limited Impact of its Implementation and Proposing Measures to Increase the Number of Mediations in the EU, 2014

Li S, Zhou G (2012) The problems of China's consumer protection law in the legal practice. Int J Bus Soc Sci 3(14) [Special Issue]:65

Sempi L, ADR and consumers between Europe and China, Op. J. Vol. 2/2011, Paper n. 5, pp. 1–14, http://lider-lab.sssup.it/opinio, online publication December 2011

Xu J, Development of ODR in China, available online at: https://law.pace.edu/lawschool/files/iicl/odr/Xu_Junke.pdf

Zhenjie H (1999), International jurisdiction of Chinese courts in contractual matters: rules, interpretation and practice. Neth Int Law Rev 46:204
Zhixiong L (2014) The recent amendment to China's consumer law: an imperfect improvement and proposal for future changes. Beijing Law Rev 5:163–171

The Law Applicable to Consumer Contracts: Protection and Gaps in China and in Europe

Nicolas Nord

The law applicable to consumer contracts is an important issue concerning the international sale of goods. Very often, the consumer contracts concern sale of goods. For example, in Europe, the idea of protection of the consumers appeared in the 1970s with the development of the mail-order selling. Of course, goods were, at this period, in concern. Nowadays, consumer contracts are much more developed, especially because of the Internet.[1] In international situations, the general conflict-of-laws rules of both systems seem to be unadapted.

The general rule according to which parties can make a choice is dangerous for the consumer. In most of the contracts, the professional will select a law, interesting for him, and the consumer has no other opportunity to accept it or to refuse the contract in general. We also know that the consumer, very often, does not read the general terms and conditions of the contract in which the choice is stipulated.

In the absence of choice, we know that the law of the habitual residence of the party whose performance of obligation is characteristic must be applied in most of the situations. This means that the law of the habitual residence of the professional is in concern. The consumer is the debtor of an obligation of payment, which is not characteristic. The solution is not the best for the consumer because he has no knowledge of such a law.

Everything is summarized in recital n°23 of Regulation Rome I: "As regards contracts concluded with parties regarded as being weaker, those parties should be protected by conflict of-law rules that are more favourable to their interests than the general rules."

This is why, in both systems, the necessity to adapt the general solutions has led to special conflict-of-law rules: 5 of the Rome Convention, Article 6 of Regulation

[1]For some observations on the impact of Internet, Smith (2000), p. 260.

N. Nord (✉)
Faculty of Law, University of Strasbourg, Strasbourg, France
e-mail: nicolas.nord@unistra.fr

N. Nord, G. Cerqueira (eds.), *International Sale of Goods*, China-EU Law Series 5,
DOI 10.1007/978-3-319-54036-8_10

Rome I in Europe, and Article 42 of the 2010 Statute in China.[2] The Hague Convention of June 15, 1955, on the Law applicable to international sales of goods contains no special conflict-of-law rule with regard to the protection of consumers. This should mean that there is lack of rules and that, in its material scope of application, the sale of goods, the special conflict-of-law rules of the Rome Convention and of Regulation Rome I must be applied. The silence of the Convention has, for example, been interpreted by the Swiss legislator as permission to create special rules for consumer contracts.[3] The same solution should be used more generally and especially for the European instruments.

The main question, common to both systems, is to identify the contracts concerned by the special rule and which ones must be submitted only to the rules of principle. We will then first study the scope of application of these rules (Sect. 1). Even if the conflictual approach is not the same in Europe and in China, some common steps can be identified (Sect. 2). Overriding mandatory provisions are also in question. Despite the existence of special rules, the exception mechanism may still be used to protect the weaker party (Sect. 3).

1 Scope of Application

In both systems, many conditions must be fulfilled to apply the special conflict-of-law rules.

1.1 In Europe

The consumer is defined (Sect. 1.1.1), and the contracts concerned are listed (Sect. 1.1.2) by Regulation Rome I.

1.1.1 The Notion of Consumer

The definition is given in the text itself. According to the first sentence of Article 6 § 1 of Regulation Rome I, "a contract concluded by a natural person for a purpose which can be regarded as being outside his trade or profession (the consumer) with another person acting in the exercise of his trade or profession (the professional)." Different elements are remarkable.

[2]For authors pleading for the introduction of such special rules before the adoption of the 2010 Statute, see Huang et al. (2008), p. 440.

[3]Art. 118 § 2 and 120 of the Federal Law on Private International Law (18 December 1987). See esp. Vischer (1992), p. 161.

Only natural persons are concerned. This means of course that companies and other legal persons can never be considered as consumers. It is essential because in other fields of EU law, some courts had hesitations on that question[4] and that, remarkably, Article 5 of the Rome Convention contains no provision about the type of person concerned.[5]

The aim of the contract is determinant. The only question is always "what has the contract been concluded for?" If it is for the trade or profession of the person concerned, then the contract cannot be considered as a consumer contract, even if he is not an expert in the field. For example, if a butcher decides to conclude a contract of installation of an alarm system in his shop, Article 6 cannot be applied due to the professional aim. The solution is the same according to Article 5 of the Rome Convention. If the contract is concluded both for personal and professional reasons, the professional side is determinant according to the solutions of the Court of Justice in the field of conflict of jurisdictions.[6]

If there is a consumer, a professional must be the other contracting party. The provisions cannot be applied for a contract concluded between two consumers because there is no need for protection. The solution appears explicitly in the Regulation and is only implicit in the Rome Convention.

1.1.2 The Contracts

It is the main evolution between Regulation Rome I and the Rome Convention.

The principle, in the Regulation, is again easy to understand: all the contracts are concerned. But five exceptions exist according to paragraph 4 of Article 6. None of them concerns the sale of goods.

The approach of the Convention is completely different. Article 5 § 1 states that the system of protection can be applied only to some contracts, especially the sale of goods, which can be considered as the essence of the consumer's contracts.[7] The contracts that are not mentioned are all excluded.

[4]For the situation and the hesitations in France, Gaudemet-Tallon, Fasc. 552-15, n°63.

[5]According to article 5§1 of the Rome Convention "*This Article applies to a contract the object of which is the supply of goods or services to a person ('the consumer') for a purpose which can be regarded as being outside his trade or profession, or a contract for the provision of credit for that object*".

[6]CJEU 20 January 2005, Gruber, C-464/01, Rec. I. 439, concl. F.G. Jacobs.

[7]"*This Article applies to a contract the object of which is the* ***supply of goods or services*** *...*". For explanations about article 5, see Giuliano and Lagarde (1980), p. 23.

1.2 *In China*

There is no definition of the consumer or of the consumer contracts in the statute itself. Some clues can nevertheless be given.

The first one is a definition of the consumer in Article 2 of the law of October 2, 1993, on the protection of the rights and interests of the consumers, according to which the consumer is "any natural person who buys and uses goods or services for her daily consumption."[8] We know that the classification is governed by the law of the forum.[9] It is then possible to consider that this definition can be used also in the field of conflict of laws, especially knowing that the article itself permits such an extension to other texts.[10] This also means that there is a real convergence between both systems. Only natural persons can be considered as consumers.

The second clue can be found in Article 42 directly, which refers to a "consumer" on the one hand and to a "business operator" on the other hand. The situation seems then to be the same as in Europe. A professional must be the other party. The contracts concluded between two natural persons acting outside the field of their trades or professions are not concerned.

The last element that must be underlined is that there is no restriction concerning the contracts themselves. All the different types are to be considered, including the sale of goods.

The scope of application is identified in both systems. A contract of sale of goods between a consumer and a professional can be submitted to the special conflict-of-law rule. The conflictual mechanism must then be studied.

2 The Conflict-of-Law Rules

In both systems, two situations are considered. The first is the absence of a choice made by the parties. A law will be objectively identified (Sect. 2.1). The second is the choice made by the parties of the law applicable to the contract. The freedom of the parties exists in Europe and in China but is not as important as for the contracts in general, due to the will to protect the consumers (Sect. 2.2).

[8]For more details, Brooke Overby (2006), p. 347.

[9]Article 8 of the Law on the laws applicable to foreign-related civil relations of 2010: "*Classification of foreign-related civil relations is governed by the law of the forum*".

[10]Cerqueira et al. (2011), p. 54.

2.1 The Law Applicable in the Absence of Choice

In both systems, the principle is the same. The law of the habitual residence of the consumer is at the first rank, but it will not be applied unconditionally.

In China, Article 42 of the Statute is in concern. It states that "A consumer contract is governed by the law of the consumer's habitual residence." But, according to the second sentence, "where the business operator does not engage in any business activity in the habitual residence of the consumer, the law of the place where the commodity or service is provided shall be applied."

In Europe, according to the first paragraph of Article 6 of Regulation Rome I, such contracts "shall be governed by the law of the country where the consumer has his habitual residence, provided that the professional:

a) pursues his commercial or professional activities in the country where the consumer has his habitual residence, or

b) by any means, directs such activities to that country or to several countries including that country, and the contract falls within the scope of such activities."

In the Rome Convention, the law of the habitual residence of the consumer will only be applied

- *if in that country the conclusion of the contract was preceded by a specific invitation addressed to him or by advertising, and he had taken in that country all the steps necessary on his part for the conclusion of the contract, or*
- *if the other party or his agent received the consumer's order in that country, or*
- *if the contract is for the sale of goods and the consumer travelled from that country to another country and there gave his order, provided that the consumer's journey was arranged by the seller for the purpose of inducing the consumer to buy.*[11]

The reasons of the convergentce of the solutions are easy to understand. The law of the habitual residence is the one that the consumer knows the best or the one he has the easiest access to.[12] The protection is then not a material one, on this step of reasoning, because the law can contain no system of protection for the consumers but just a conflictual one.

However, the interests of the professional are also taken into consideration. The main idea is that he must not be surprised by the application of the law of the residence of the consumer. Two different ways exists, but the general idea is the same.

In China, the activity of the professional is in concern. If he is not engaged in activities in the country of the habitual residence of the consumer, this law will not be applied. The reason is that he cannot reasonably expect the application of that law. It is not predictable for him.[13] He has not accepted to take the risk of the

[11] Article 5 §2 and 3.

[12] Alexandre (2011), p. 114; Huo (2011), p. 1087.

[13] Tu (2011), p. 581.

application of such a law by developing his activities in that country. An example permits to illustrate the solution. The professional is a Chinese firm. A contract is concluded with a French tourist, who lives in France, during his stay in China. The Chinese firm has only activities in China and different countries in Asia but none in Europe. In case of litigation about the product in question, the applicable law would be the French one. It would be a very bad solution, of course not for the consumer but for the conflictual system in general. A careful firm should therefore make a selection between the clients and check each time from which country they come. This is possible for activities online. It can be easy to refuse access to the website for persons whose residence is in a country in which a firm does not want to develop its activities. For physical trade with consumers, it is much more difficult of course. It must also be underlined that the behavior of the consumer is not taken into account in this system, even if it is his protection that is concerned.

In Europe, the solutions are based on the same approach as in the Chinese system. A link needs to be demonstrated with the country of the habitual residence of the consumer so that the application of the law of that country cannot be considered as a surprise to the professional. The criteria used by the Rome Convention seem to be irrelevant, especially with the development of the e-commerce. This is true, for example, for the specific invitation addressed to the consumer. This is why the system has been modernized by Regulation Rome I. According to recital n°24 of Regulation Rome I, "[w]ith more specific reference to consumer contracts, the conflict-of-law rule should make it possible to cut the cost of settling disputes concerning what are commonly relatively small claims and to take account of the development of distance-selling techniques." The objectives are given. We will see if they are reached by the text.

This time the application of the law of the habitual residence of the consumer depends on two positive conditions, in relation, again, to the activity of the professional. The first condition is that the professional "pursues his commercial or professional activities in the country where the consumer has his habitual residence." The second alternative condition is that he "by any means, directs such activities to that country or to several countries including that country." In both situations, the contract needs to fall within the scope of his professional activities.

The first situation concerns the "classical" activity of trade in a country. The second expression refers to the electronic commerce and repeats the terms of Regulations n°44/2001 "Brussels I" and n°1215/2012 "Brussels I *bis*."

The system, again, tries to protect the consumer, but not to submit the professional to rules unexpected because his activity was not directed to the State of the habitual residence of the consumer.

According to recital n°24 of Regulation Rome I, the notion of "direction of activities" should "be interpreted harmoniously in Regulation (EC) n°44/2001 and this Regulation, bearing in mind that a joint declaration by the Council and the Commission on Article 15 of Regulation (EC) n°44/2001 states that 'for Article 15 (1)I to be applicable it is not sufficient for an undertaking to target its activities at the Member State of the consumer's residence, or at a number of Member States including that Member State; a contract must also be concluded within the framework of its activities'. The declaration also states that 'the mere fact that an Internet site is accessible is not sufficient for Article 15 to be applicable, although a factor will be that this Internet site solicits the conclusion of distance contracts and that a contract has actually been concluded at a distance, by whatever means. In this respect, the language or currency which a website uses does not constitute a relevant factor."

This means that the notion of direction of activities must be interpreted as it has already been done in the field of conflict of jurisdictions by the Court of Justice, especially in the *Pammer and Alpenhof* case.[14]

In both systems, if the conditions are not fulfilled, the general provision must be applied, Article 4 of Regulation Rome I or Article 41 of the 2010 Statute, articles that we already know.[15]

2.2 *The Possibility to Choose the Applicable Law*

In China and in Europe, the law applicable to the consumers' contracts can be chosen by the parties. The general conflict-of-law rule is not ousted, which would have been a solution to protect the consumer. Indeed, the result is that very often the law will be imposed by the professional. The consumer has only one option: agreeing to the choice or refusing, which means that the contract will not be concluded. There are no negotiations in practice on this point, as for the others. This is especially true for contracts concluded on the Internet. The consumer will give his agreement to the standard terms and conditions of sale online. It will not be possible for him to enter in a discussion with the professional.

An application of the general solution is then not opportune. A protection of the consumer is highly desirable. A concrete application is found in article 6 § 2 of Regulation Rome I, which introduces a limit to the choice. It states in the first sentence that "the parties may choose the law applicable to a contract which fulfils the requirements of paragraph 1, in accordance with Article 3." It is a free choice. The law chosen can have no link with the contract. But according to the second sentence, "Such a choice may not, however, have the result of depriving the consumer of the protection afforded to him by provisions that cannot be derogated from by agreement by virtue of the law which, in the absence of choice, would have been applicable on the basis of paragraph 1." The same rule can be found in Article 5 § 2 of the Rome Convention. The situation of the consumer cannot get worse due to the choice. The provisions that cannot be derogated from by agreement of the law applicable according to paragraph 1 are a limit. The law chosen will either be

[14]See in this book, Alexandre, Identification of the competent judge in China and in Europe—European solutions.

[15]See in this book, Nord, Identification of the applicable law in China and in Europe.

neutral or improve his protection. Of course, the conflict-of-law rule is not a real guarantee for the consumer. Everything depends on the level of protection of the law of the habitual residence of the consumer. Different situations exist and show the limits of the approach: if the law of its habitual residence is not protective and there is no choice, if the law of its habitual residence is chosen and is not protective, if the laws of the habitual residence and the one chosen are not protective at all, and so forth.

Another point must be underlined: the solution can be difficult to use in practice. It imposes a comparison between the provisions of two laws. At least one of them will be unknown for the judge. But above all, such an approach can lead to the application of two laws to the same contract.[16] The comparison does not seem to be a general one. If the law chosen is less protective than the law of the habitual residence of the consumer about one point, it must be ousted for the question concerned. But if it is more favorable about the other points, it will be applied for them. The solution is then very complicated for the judge and also unreadable in advance for the parties.

In the Chinese system, the solution is different. Article 42 of the Statute states in its second sentence that "Where the consumer chooses the law of the place where the commodity or the service is provided [...] the law of the place where the commodity or service is provided shall be applied." A limited possibility of choice exists then, and it is reserved to the consumer. It is not as in Europe a choice made by both parties but only by the weakest one.[17] However, this mechanism also reflects, in a different way, the will to protect the weaker party.

The solution seems to be surprising, but the Chinese law is not isolated. The Japanese Statute of private international law (*Horei*) of 2006 uses also a one-side choice about consumer contracts in its Article 11, even if the rules are different.[18]

The interests of the professional are also taken into account because the alternative law that may be chosen by the consumer cannot be a surprise to him.[19] The law of the place where the commodity is provided has a strong link with the contract, and the possibility to apply it is highly justified.

The solution can be easily admitted by both parties. The following example can be imagined. A Chinese consumer, who has his habitual residence in China, buys goods sold by a French firm via the Internet. The place of delivery is in Vietnam where the consumer has a holiday residence. The French firm admits to organize this delivery. The consumer will have the opportunity to choose between the application of the Chinese and the Vietnamese laws. He will of course choose the law that is more beneficial to him. The French firm cannot be surprised due to the admission to develop its activities in these two countries.

---

[16] Underlying the problems, Brand (2013), p. 194.

[17] For an explanation of the mechanism, Pissler (2012), p. 33.

[18] See Nishitani (2008), p. 94.

[19] Mellone and Nord (2013), p. 168.

The solution leads also to the exclusive application of one law. There is no possibility of combination between two laws, unlike what prevails in Europe. The Chinese approach seems to be easier to deal with in practice and much more satisfying concerning this particular point.

One question still remains, however: how will the place where the commodity is provided be determined? The confusion between a legal or a material approach is possible. Even if a material one is chosen, problems can still occur, for example, in situations in which the contract is not executed. The European experience in the field of conflict of jurisdictions about the issue of competence in contractual matters is not necessarily the best concerning the determination of the place of performance.[20]

3 The Overriding Mandatory Provisions

The main question is to know if it is possible to apply this mechanism in the field of the consumer contracts, especially to protect the consumer.

In Europe, there have been many discussions about this question. In some countries, mandatory provisions have been used to protect the consumer, especially in situations in which the special conflict-of-law rule was not applicable. In France, for example, the *Cour de cassation* has used many times the mechanism to apply the French law and so to protect the consumer.[21]

In Germany, the *Bundesgerichtshof* has decided that it was not possible to use mandatory provisions to protect the consumer.[22] He will be either protected by the special conflict-of-law rule or submitted to the general solutions, Articles 3 and 4 of the Rome Convention and Regulation Rome I. A compromise is not possible. The justification of this hard solution for the consumer is that the conflict-of-law rule is a special clause of application of mandatory provisions that ousts the general clause.

Of course, these solutions are now less important because the Regulation has adopted a wider approach concerning the contracts included in the special rule than the Convention. As we know, the principle is that all the contracts are concerned.

[20]Article 5-1 of the Brussels Convention and the regulation Brussels I, article 7-1 of the regulation Brussels I *bis*. See Chapter I, Section I—International sale of goods and identification of the competent judge in China and in Europe.

[21]For examples: see Civ. 1st 19 October 1999, *Rev. crit.* 2000, 29, n. P. Lagarde ; *D.* 2000, p. 8, obs. J. F. ; *JDI* 2000, 328, n. J.-B. Racine; *D.* 2000, 765, n. M. Audit; Civ. 1st 10 July 2001, Bull. civ. I, n°210; 23 May 2006, Bull. civ. I, n°258; R., p. 465; D. 2006. 2798, n. M. Audit; D. 2007. Pan. 1754, obs. P. Courbe and 2567, obs. S. Bollée; CCE 2006, n° 143, note C. Chabert; Dr. et patr. December 2006, p. 80, obs. M.-E. Ancel; RDC 2006. 1253, obs. P. Deumier; *Rev. crit. DIP* 2007. 85, n. D. Cocteau-Senn. For general comments, Vareilles-Sommières de (2006), p. 2464.

[22]BGH 2 October 1993, *IPRax* 1994, 449 and 19 March 1997, *Rev. crit. DIP* 1998, 610, n. P. Lagarde.

In China, the 2012 interpretation of the Chinese Supreme Court is again useful.[23] A list of matters in which the mechanism of mandatory provisions can be used to apply the Chinese law is contained in Article 10. The protection of the consumer is not directly mentioned. Indirectly, some provisions could have an impact. This is especially true for the second category mentioned according to which the mechanism can be used when "the product safety or the safety of public health is concerned." It is a crucial issue in China as we all know and can affect the law that is normally applicable to consumer contracts.

The main question is to know if the mechanism can also be used to protect directly the consumer. The list given by the Supreme Court is not exhaustive, and mandatory provisions can be used also in other situations. The problem is then the same as in Europe. Can the general provision be used in situations in which a protection is already given to the weaker party by the existence of a special conflict-of-law rule?

A clear difference must be underlined between both systems. In Europe, the mandatory provisions are at the origin of the system of protection introduced in the Convention and the Regulation. The law of the habitual residence of the consumer has been considered as mandatory by several decisions in different European countries. The Convention and the Regulation have then changed the approach and transformed the reasoning.[24] It is no more necessary to use an exception mechanism. The protection of the consumer is now provided by the conflict-of-law rule directly. But a paternity exists between both of them, and the imperativity of the rules of the habitual residence can still be found in Articles 5 of the Convention and 6 of the Regulation. The law chosen by the parties is ousted only if the level of protection is lower than according to the provisions that cannot be derogated from by agreement by virtue of the law of the habitual residence. A comparison must be made.

In China, the solution is different despite the will to protect the consumer. There is no reference to the imperativity of the rules of the law of the habitual residence. There is an alternativity between two laws, and the protection is provided by the unilateralization of the choice, reserved to the consumer. The mechanism of mandatory provisions is not at the origin of the reasoning. This means that there is no competition between a special and a general clause. The consumer could then be protected by application of Chinese mandatory provisions. Such a situation can occur when the law of the place where the commodity is provided is applied because the business operator does not engage in any business activity in the habitual residence of the consumer.

[23]For the notion of Overriding Mandatory Provisions in China, Molerus and Nord (2011), p. 133; Xu (1997), p. 186.

[24]For a description of the evolution, see Lagarde (2001), p. 511.

4 Conclusion

The consumer is protected in both private international law systems, for international contracts of sale of goods, even if the conflictual approach is not the same. The interests of the professional are also each time taken into account. Of course, the material protection depends on the solution contained in the law or the laws that will be finally applied. The protection in private international law is very satisfying due to the specificity of such contracts but is always just the first step of the reasoning.

References

Alexandre D (2011) Conflict of law rules and the protection of the weaker party in EU private international law and in Chinese new private international law: consumer contracts and employment contracts. Chin Yearb Private Int Law Comp Law 14:102–124

Brand RA (2013) Transaction planning using rules on jurisdiction and the recognition and enforcement of judgments. Collect Courses Hague Acad Int Law 358:9–262

Brooke Overby A (2006) Consumer protection in China after accession to the WTO. Syracuse J Int Law Commer 33(2):347–392

Cerqueira G, Nord N, Porcheron D (2011) Les nouvelles règles de conflit de lois chinoises en matière contractuelle. Rev Lamy dr Aff 61:52–56

Gaudemet-Tallon H JurisClasseur Droit international, Fasc. 552–15: Convention de Rome du 19 juin 1980 et Règlement "Rome I″ du 17 juin 2008. Détermination de la loi applicable. Domaine de la loi applicable.

Giuliano M, Lagarde P (1980) Report on the Convention on the law applicable to contractual obligations. Off J Eur Commun C 282, 31/10/1980:1–50

Huang J, Hu W, Wang Q (2008) Annual survey of judicial practice in chinese private international law in 2007. Chin Yearb Comp Private Int Law 11:433–453

Huo Z (2011) An imperfect improvement: the new conflict-of-laws act of the People's Republic of China. Int Comp Law Q 60:1065–1093

Lagarde P (2001) Heurs et malheurs de la protection internationale du consommateur dans l'Union européenne. Le contrat au début du XXIème siècle, Etudes offertes à J. Ghestin. LGDJ, Paris, pp 511–526.

Mellone M, Nord N (2013) The influence of the European Union private international law on the new chinese conflict of Laws statute. PKU Int Comp Law Rev 10:141–182

Molerus L, Nord N (2011) Exceptions based on public policy and overriding mandatory provisions in EU and chinese PIL. Chin Yearb Private Int Law Comp Law 14:133–157

Nishitani Y (2008) Party autonomy and its restrictions by mandatory rules in Japanese private international law. In: Basedow J, Baum H, Nishitani Y (eds) Japanese and European private international law in comparative perspective. Mohr Siebeck, Tübingen, pp 77–104

Pissler K (2012) Das neue Internationale Privatrecht der Volksrepublik China: Nach den Steinen tastend den Fluss überqueren. RabelsZ 76:1–46

Smith BL (2000) The third industrial revolution: law and policy for the internet. Collect Courses Hague Acad Int Law 282:229–464

Tu G (2011) China's new conflicts code: general issues and selected topics. Am J Comp Law 59 (2):563–590

Vareilles-Sommières de P (2006) Le sort de la théorie des clauses spéciales d'application des lois de police en droit des contrats internationaux de consommation (nature de l'article 5 de la Convention de Rome). Recueil Dalloz:2464–2469

Vischer F (1992) General course on private international law. Collect Courses Hague Acad Int Law 232:9–255

Xu D (1997) Le droit international privé en chine: Une perspective comparative. Collect Courses Hague Acad Int Law 270:107–235

MIX
Papier aus verantwortungsvollen Quellen
Paper from responsible sources
FSC® C105338

If you have any concerns about our products,
you can contact us on
ProductSafety@springernature.com

In case Publisher is established outside the EU,
the EU authorized representative is:
Springer Nature Customer Service Center GmbH
Europaplatz 3, 69115 Heidelberg, Germany

Printed by Libri Plureos GmbH
in Hamburg, Germany